FREE TO EAT

The Proven Recipe for Permanent Weight Loss

by Bronwyn Schweigerdt, M.S.
with Natural Chef Jennifer Brewer

Peripety Media

FREE TO EAT: The Proven Recipe for Permanent Weight Loss

Copyright ©2010 Bronwyn Schweigerdt
1st ed.

Recipes and Meal Plan by Jennifer Brewer
     www.nourishingnutrition.com
Cover Design and Interior Graphics by Chrys Goodman
     www.chrysgoodman.com
Comic Cover Art by Jay French
     www.jayfrenchstudios.com

ISBN-13: 978-0-615-30609-4

Library of Congress Control Number: 2009933235

Printed and bound in the United States of America.

Packaged by Peripety Media
1501 34th St.
Sacramento, CA 96816

Quantity discounts are available on bulk purchases of this book for educational, charitable, or promotional use. Please contact Peripety Media at the address above or visit the www.fiber-girl.com website for information.

Dedication

I dedicate this book to my Abba, who gives me wisdom to understand the science of nutrition, as well as wisdom that leads to peace, joy and freedom. I am my Beloved's and You are mine. You make all things new – even me.

I want to thank my husband, Steve, who has proven to be far more than a husband and friend during the undertaking of this book. Steve, I've always heard you were amazing from your co-workers, but now I know you are quite possibly the best steward of time and energy in the world. I wrote this book, but you have done the hard part: editing, designing the cover and graphics, working with others involved, finding the best printer, and overall learning how to publish a book in three weeks. You are my manager, agent, and biggest support. Thank you. I love you.

Also, thank you to all those who have encouraged me to write another weight loss and nutrition book. To my almost-literary agent Susan Schulman, who believed in this work from the first paragraph and helped me develop its course over an entire year. To my blog readers who have been with me along this journey, letting me know the world needs this book. And to all the wonderful people who have attended my seminars over the years, asking great questions and sharing your success stories with me. Each and every story strengthens my drive to help more people live longer and better.

And to you dear Reader. Ultimately, I dedicate this book to you. May you be inspired and persuaded by what you read that you can lose weight permanently, get off your medications (or never need any), and live a long and abundant life. You are the only person who can nourish you, and my prayer is that you learn how – and do it. The world needs the best of you.

May you live long, be blessed, and be free to eat.

Pat's Story

I had allowed the busyness of life to take priority over my health. My weight had climbed to an all time high. I had wrestled with a tangle of weight loss books in the past that emphasized no carb diets, low carb diets, and low fat diets. I asked myself, "How do you struggle through the web of misinformation and get to the truth of healthy eating for life and weight loss?"

Then I picked up Bronwyn's first little weight loss book *The UnDiet*. I slowly and gently applied one principle at a time, from January 2008 to May 2008, allowing myself a full month to adjust to each change. During this time I lost 50 pounds and kept the weight off for over one year. I lost the weight so quickly some people swore that I had undergone gastric bypass surgery!

Not only have I kept the weight off for well over a year, but I am still slowly losing weight. Applying these four eating principles was easy: I was always full, and I know that I have made some habits that will last the rest of my life.

So to pay it forward, I would love to share these principles (and my experience) with you.

How I Switched to Drinking Water, Not Calories

I began by replacing all calorie containing drinks with water and "Good Earth" tea. Even though I typically would add a little milk and sugar or Splenda to my tea, the "Good Earth" brand of cinnamon tea is sweet without adding sugar. Thus, I was merely drinking "naturally flavored water".

I also started bringing a 32-ounce water bottle to work which I would fill up at the water cooler as soon as I got to the office (on the weekends I would fill the bottle as soon as I was up for the day). Just before my second meal, I would refill the water bottle. It took about 10 to 15 days to get used to drinking six glasses of water a day, and another 2-3 weeks to get up to eight glasses.

Periodically I would still have my beloved mocha, but I took baby steps to slowly eliminate them from my routine. I started by switching from a 24 ounce decaf mocha to a 16 ounce and cut down to two mochas a week. The second week I left off the whipped cream and switched to a 12 ounce, but still drank two mochas a week. During the third week, I cut down to one mocha and I replaced the 2 percent milk with soymilk, which also added 3 grams of fiber! The fourth week I switched from a 12 ounce decaf mocha to an 8 ounce.

By the fifth week, I went to get my weekly mocha treat, took one sip, and actually threw the rest in the trash because I realized that I did not want it. As I lost weight, the desire for the sweets decreased because weight loss became, in effect, its own sweet reward. I still go to coffee, but if I want a drink I choose the Banana Chocolate Vivano as a meal replacement following a strenuous workout, or I have a decaf Americano.

Increasing my water intake substantially decreased my hunger and improved the appearance of my skin. The pores on my face tightened creating a finer texture that others soon noticed. Many women and even some men asked me if I had changed make-up brands.

The best part of drinking water is that I crave water now. While I prefer the taste of bottled water, my body does not have a preference and I will often drink tap water if bottled water is not available. The cooler the water the better. Just thinking about hot, humid summers and drinking cool water from the hose makes me thirsty. As soon as I realized that drinking water was a habit, I took another baby step.

Learning to Eat Only When Hungry

Learning to eat only when I was hungry was the most difficult principle to implement. However, to lose the weight and keep it off I knew I had to do it. While trying to instill this habit, I realized that my eating had been driven by something other than physical hunger for quite some time. Despite my best efforts, I struggled with developing this habit. I made multiple attempts and failed, but I knew my tenacity and discipline would be rewarded.

Finally, I tried to keep a food diary on a Post-It note each day. Prior to consuming a meal or snack (and consume I did back then), I wrote down the time I ate, what I ate, when I ate, who I was with, and how I ate (quickly, slowly, sitting, standing). A very dysfunctional eating pattern emerged over only a few days.

I discovered that I ate according to the clock, and not based on physical hunger. Meals consisted of substantial amounts of protein, low carbohydrates (I barely ate fiber), and were low in fat. All of my lunches were eaten at my desk while working so that food became associated with work. To compound matters, I ate almost all of my meals alone. To my dismay, I discovered that I ate my meals very quickly which prevented me from recognizing when my hunger was satisfied. Finally, I would often skip meals and consume a "super meal" just after work with vast amounts of calories and the food was practically shoveled into my mouth at the kitchen counter.

To learn to recognize hunger, I agreed to only eat food that I enjoyed, which often required that I season the food and prepare my own meals. During this time, I threw out a lot of food as I rediscovered what foods I liked and disliked. I learned that much of what I ate was tasteless, and in retrospect, I ate these foods without enjoying them. Often I overate to try to satisfy my starving taste buds.

I now refuse to eat food that does not taste delicious. I have also cultivated a habit of eating many herbs with my meals. I love fresh basil on a veggie sandwich, cilantro with yogurt, parsley with most anything and of course, all of these and more with a hot meal.

When food began tasting better, I ate more slowly because I actually wanted to savor the taste of the food. I had an unexpected outcome - I was often unable to finish my meal without feeling stuffed. I began to wrap the leftovers for later. After about a week of this, I began to notice a growling in my stomach that did not stop when I drank my water or hot tea. I realized I was hungry and so I would take out the leftovers from my last meal and finish them.

Filling Up on Fiber

I eat a minimum of 35-40 grams of fiber each day. To retrain myself, I began eating some fiber at every meal so that I could feel satiated (full), spaced my meals out every four hours to start, committed to not missing meals, and promised not to eat at my desk.

I immediately noticed that I was hungry less often and I was able to decrease the size of many of my meals to less than half of what they were. In fact, I often eat my meals off a salad plate or even a saucer. As I increased my fiber, I noticed an unfortunate outcome…I was becoming constipated and my stomach seemed a little bloated. As Bronwyn teaches, fiber needs water to move, so I began to drink water at the end of my meals. Problem solved! In addition, I noticed that my abdomen actually got flatter after I increased the fiber in my diet (over the course of about two to three weeks).

Eating Smaller, More Frequent Meals

The combination of drinking water, increasing fiber and eating only when I was hungry naturally resulted in my body demanding smaller, more frequent meals or snacks. One unexpected outcome is that I am ravenous when I wake up in the morning. But since that means my metabolism is higher, I know this is a good thing. I now eat five to six meals/snacks a day depending upon what I eat and how much I exercise. During this time, I learned that I often would want to eat when stressed at work even if I was not hungry.

Food is for the enjoyment and nourishment of the body. Through Bronwyn's principles, I learned how to reclaim the simple joy of eating while nourishing my body. By following these tips, you can eat a healthier diet while learning how to savor your meals. It takes a while to re-establish a taste for what is wholesome and natural.

Fifty-something pounds later, I can honestly say making these changes was truly painless, and I am never hungry.

Here are some encouragements and suggestions for your journey:

1) Food should satisfy your taste buds and your hunger. Learn to season your food to make sure that your taste buds are satisfied.

2) It takes about 30 days to replace an unhealthy habit with a healthy one, so learn to be patient with yourself. If you fail one day, start again the next day. Eventually the time between failures will increase and you will have established a habit.

3) This is not a diet! It is a lifestyle change and changes take time, so be kind to yourself!

4) Everything that I eat or drink that contains calories (i.e., nutrients) also has at least 3 grams of fiber.

5)   Alleviate and deal with your stress. This will prevent you from "stress eating".

I did have one negative outcome from applying Bronwyn's principles... I had to buy new wardrobe 4 sizes smaller! Bronwyn's advice on healthy eating is solid and I have made it my personal goal to see her on Oprah some day soon.

Pat Sherard, 43, Program Manager

Contents

PART TWO: RECIPES AND MEAL PLAN

Confessions of a Nutritionist

I don't want to brag, but I happen to be an expert in weight loss. (Boy, that does sound like bragging, though!) It's not just that I am slender, which I am, but through my previous book, *The UnDiet* and weight loss seminars, I've been able to help thousands of other people lose weight. In fact, one of my life ambitions is to free millions of people to eat great tasting foods that help them get healthy.

That may sound overly ambitious, but most people are overweight and tired for one major reason: lack of information. Or more accurately: misinformation. You may think the problem is a lack of resolve, low willpower, and a society that produces too much processed food in portions that are too big. And that's true. But people know about that. You'd be surprised at what folks — even you — don't know.

I have a Master's of Science degree in nutrition from the world's most renowned school of nutrition: Tufts University. Yet I didn't realize the power of these nutrition principles until I taught about it in my college nutrition classes. Students came up to me at the end of the semester telling me they'd lost fifteen pounds or more during my class, their cholesterol had gone down, their blood pressure was under control. Some were even taken off medication for diabetes and high blood pressure. I heard the same claims semester after semester.

This prompted me to self-publish my first book, *The UnDiet: Painless Baby Steps to Permanent Weight Loss.* I started giving seminars all over the country. I heard stories of people who had struggled all their lives with their weight but lost fifty or more pounds on this new eating plan. These people were excited, because this was no short-term "quick fix." It was something they could do for the rest of their lives.

I recently received a thank you card from a former nutrition student. Her name is Judi and she is preparing for retirement. One of her concerns as a single woman with no children is being healthy enough to qualify for retirement benefits. When she enrolled in my class, based on her health indicators, she was not able to qualify. In her card, she told me that after having high blood pressure for seven years, her doctor just took her off medication completely. Judi's blood pressure is in a healthy range, she is 35 pounds lighter and for the first time in almost 40 years, she no longer experiences sinus headaches. Needless to say, now she will receive medical benefits after she retires.

In fact, my favorite testimonials are from senior citizens. Most of us believe growing old automatically means weight gain and chronic disease – but these folks show us otherwise. If seniors can lose weight and turn their health around, anyone can. For instance, during a two-month-long nutrition course I taught one older gentleman lost 40 pounds. He told his wife he couldn't believe he was losing weight, since he never felt hungry or deprived. In the same class, one 70-year-old woman was able to discontinue her blood pressure medication (she had been taking it for 10 years), and another elderly woman was taken off insulin for her Type II Diabetes.

Then there's me.

During college I was a little big. Pleasantly plump, some would say. I exercised like a madwoman to keep extra weight at bay. But it wasn't until years later, when I started applying my knowledge, that I saw the light. And weight disappeared: fifteen pounds over the course of one year. I also have tons more energy, longer endurance, and even a better memory. That's because I'm eating the way my body was designed to eat. I'm consuming lots of fiber as well as nutrients, antioxidants, and healthy fats like Omega-3 fatty acids. And most importantly, I only eat stuff that tastes really good. And so will you.

You will find following the principles in to *Free to Eat* will cause a steady weight loss for years to come. Prepare to feel better than you have in a long time and to look the best you ever have. In fact, if you want to shock (in a good way) old friends at your high school reunions, *Free to Eat* is the eating plan you've been waiting for.

PART ONE: Free to Eat

HAPPY MATH

People are not fat because they eat too much, but because they retain too many calories. There's a difference. You've probably heard the universal weight-loss equation: Calories In minus Calories Out equal Calories Stored, or Fat. Many of us are borderline-obsessive about counting calories, carbs, fat or all three. But we've simply been focusing on the wrong part of the equation.

Fiber is a carbohydrate contained in food that, unlike starch and sugar carbs, is indigestible in humans. That means the foods we eat that are comprised of fiber (think bean burrito, not Metamucil, which is a supplement rather than a food) cannot be broken down or absorbed by the body. As soluble fiber in food binds with water in our stomachs and expands, we feel full. This sensation regulates our blood sugar, thus preventing insulin resistance and excessive hunger. Then fiber calories go out the back door and flush, they're gone.

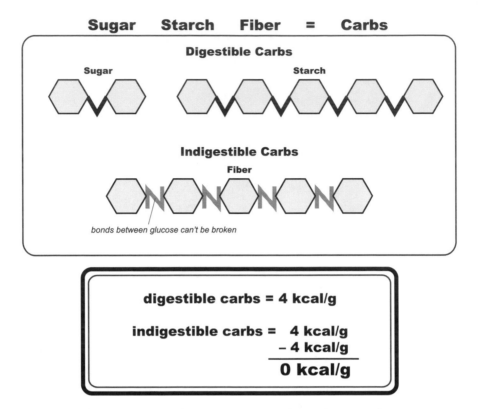

Every gram of fiber we eat in food burns about seven calories while our digestive tract processes it. So if you're consuming a typical American diet comprised of twelve grams of fiber or less (often much less), you can burn more calories just by eating more strategically.

Our bodies produce hormones when enough high-fiber foods are eaten on a regular basis. Studies show these hormones can curb even the most voracious appetites, causing significant weight loss.[1] We were not designed to retain all the calories the typical American adult consumes. This is evidenced by the rising epidemic of colon disorders and type II diabetes.

So I don't care how many times you've heard it: All calories are *not* equal. If you eat a one-hundred-calorie apple, you assume that you're consuming one hundred calories. But that apple contains five grams of fiber, and that fiber has four calories per gram that are not digested or absorbed in humans. So you can actually subtract twenty calories (4 calories per gram times 5 grams) from the original one hundred. Each gram of fiber causes your body to burn seven calories, so metabolism negates thirty-five more calories (5 grams of fiber times 7 calories per gram), giving you a net retention of only forty-five calories from your one-hundred-calorie apple.

Now let's contrast that apple with a one-hundred-calorie pack of cookies. Most cookies have almost no fiber. That means we retain each and every one of those hundred calories. Not to mention the fact that cookies don't make us feel nearly as full or produce any appetite-controlling hormones. On the contrary, the artificial flavors in most cookies will make you crave more food.

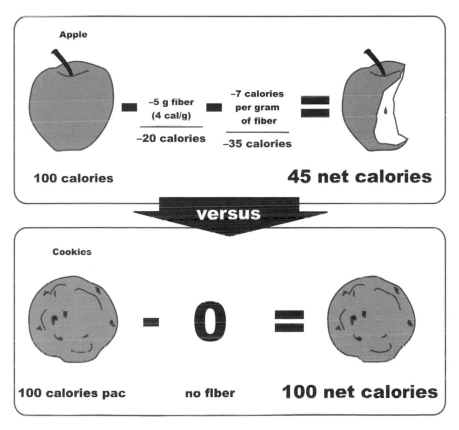

Is one hundred calories simply one hundred calories? Hardly.

A typical American diet consists of two thousand calories, with perhaps ten grams of fiber. If we subtract forty calories for the four indigestible calories per gram of fiber, then another seventy calories for the increased metabolism of that fiber, we can subtract one hundred and ten calories total. In other words, the typical American eats two thousand calories and retains almost all of them (1,890 calories).

Let's say you eat two thousand calories throughout the day. But you also eat forty grams of fiber. If you multiply forty grams times four calories per gram, then subtract those 160 calories, you only retained 1,880 calories. Since each gram of fiber you consume burns seven calories, you can multiply forty by seven and subtract 280 more calories, leaving you with a net intake of only 1,560 of those two thousand calories.

Remember that old adage "You are what you eat"? Clearly, that's only half the story. Limiting your calories results in a loss of energy and an increase in hunger. But by increasing your fiber intake, you can eat more but retain far less. Now that's happy math.

When most of us think of carbs, we think of sugar or starch. And while we need sugars and starches in order to survive (our brain cells are fueled by them), we also need plenty of fiber to regulate our blood sugar. Because it is an indigestible carbohydrate, fiber works to slow the release of other carbs into our blood stream. So we are much less likely to develop diabetes, or even continue to have diabetes, if we eat a high-fiber diet regularly. (We're also less likely to be moody and hungry when our blood sugar is stable – how awesome is that?).

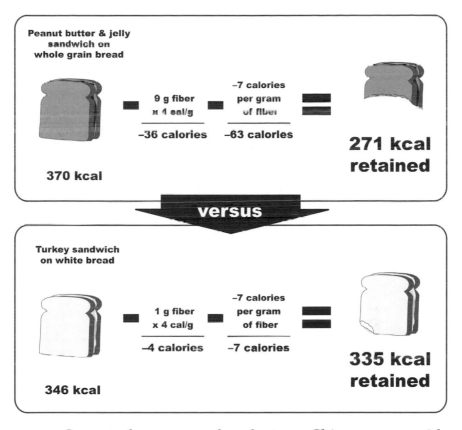

Peanut butter & jelly sandwich on whole grain bread

370 kcal − 9 g fiber x 4 cal/g (−36 calories) − −7 calories per gram of fiber (−63 calories) = **271 kcal retained**

versus

Turkey sandwich on white bread

346 kcal − 1 g fiber x 4 cal/g (−4 calories) − −7 calories per gram of fiber (−7 calories) = **335 kcal retained**

One study compared sedentary Chinese men with sedentary American men. As you might have guessed, the Chinese men had an average body weight (for height) 20 percent lower than the American men. Yet the Chinese men ate 30 percent more calories per day (per kilogram body weight) than the Americans. How? You guessed it: the Chinese guys were eating lots of fiber: thirty-three grams a day on average, compared to the Americans at eleven grams.[2]

Another study entitled "Increasing Total Fiber Intake Reduces Risk of Weight and Fat Gains in Women" was published in the Journal of Nutrition. In the study, 252 women were tracked for 20 months. Researchers found that the women who consumed the most fiber were the least likely to gain weight over the study period (almost 50% of the women gained weight and fat during the 20 months). In fact, the statistical analysis showed for every 1 gram increase in dietary fiber consumed, weight decreased by .25 kg and body fat decreased by .25 percentage points. This was even true when the study accounted for physical activity and dietary fat intake.[3]

Need more convincing? Another ten-year study that followed 2900 adults found that those who ate about 21 grams of fiber per day (based on 2,000 calories per day) weighed an average of eight pounds less than those who did not.[4] Just think about how good those people felt at their high school reunions. And imagine how they would have looked if they ate 40 grams of fiber a day.

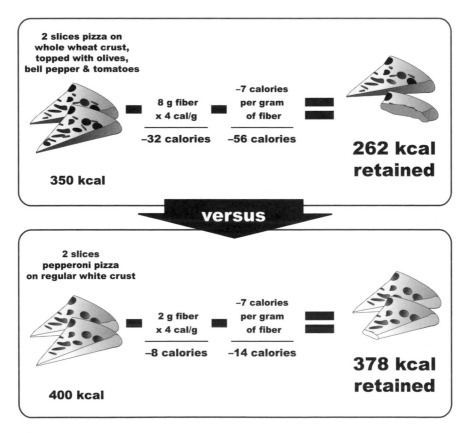

SUPERHERO CALORIES

Now let's consider the "Calories Out" part of the equation. Most people think this refers solely to exercise. By limiting our calories and exercising more, we may lose weight, but we will also become hungry. Our hunger will cause us to feel deprived, and we all know how long that kind of weight loss lasts.

You might be so disciplined that you can actually stick to a calorie- (or carb- or fat-) restricted diet. You might go to your grave looking pretty good. But chances are you will have lived your life as a moody, obsessive person and no one will come to your funeral. I mean, who wants to be around someone who is on an endless diet? We want it all – to look good and have people love us. So let's quit with the diets already.

When we realize that fiber increases our Calories Out, we can stop obsessing about Calories In. Then we can relax, enjoy our food, and eat freely.

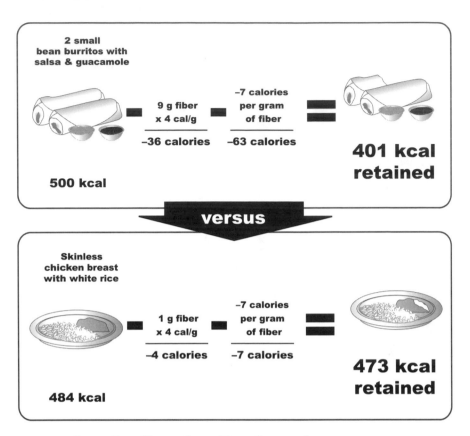

How Our Bodies Are Designed

Obesity in our culture is not primarily a result of eating too much. That is part of the problem, but not the root. Ultimately, Americans are retaining too many calories. We are eating low-fiber diets that result not only in becoming overweight but in developing colon diseases and diabetes.

Our bodies are designed to consume lots of food but not to keep all the calories. We are made to run best on twenty-five to forty grams of high-fiber foods a day. When I share this in my seminars, most people think, "There's no way I could eat that much fiber regularly – that's why I take a supplement." Although fiber supplement companies have been very successful at convincing us it is nearly impossible – and miserable – to eat a high fiber diet, don't let them fool you.

Fiber is found not just in fruit, vegetables and whole grains, but in legumes. Legumes are the easiest way to increase fiber: they consist of all the beans (except jelly beans), lentils, peas, nuts and seeds. For instance, if you were to take a cup of pistachios with you to work one morning and graze on them throughout the day, you would have consumed 14 grams of fiber – and probably loved every minute of it! Add to that a bowl of split pea soup for dinner, and you have 7 more grams of fiber – you're already nearing your goal of 25-40 grams! Other delicious foods like avocados, guacamole, almonds and peanut butter, apples, oranges, artichoke hearts, popcorn, dried apricots, lentil soup, falafel and hummus, and bean burritos are all very high in fiber. (An exhaustive list of high-fiber foods is found in the appendix, just waiting to be discovered.)

Diabetes

Fiber is critical for combating diabetes because it slows the rate of glucose absorption. What is important is not the amount of sugar or starch in a food, but the amount of fiber since that determines the rate at which sugar is digested. Thus, a low-fiber food (like white rice) will have a much faster rate of glucose absorption than a high-fiber food (like brown rice). A low-fiber food will cause blood sugar to spike and fall quickly, whereas a higher-fiber food makes glucose climb slowly, stay within healthy parameters for a longer period, and lower slowly.

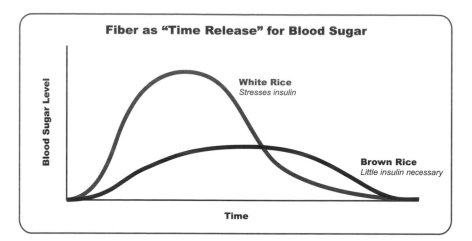

Eating low-fiber foods day in and day out taxes the body's insulin. Over time, this will lead to insulin resistance. With a high-fiber diet, insulin doesn't have to work so hard. The fiber acts as a "time release" for blood sugar by slowing the release from the stomach to the intestines, so there's never too much glucose for insulin to deal with at once.

One study put thirteen men with type II diabetes on a "high-fiber" diet for two weeks. At the end of the 14 days, nine men were able to discontinue insulin and other drugs taken for diabetes. Another man only required half the amount of insulin. Blood glucose was significantly lower in all 10 men, as were cholesterol and triglyceride levels.[1] In a study on Type I diabetics, those following a high fiber diet significantly reduced mean daily blood glucose concentrations and the number of hypoglycemic events.[2]

A hospital dietician once told me that dieticians, for the most part, do not teach patients who are diabetic about the Glycemic Index, which distinguishes between high- and low-fiber foods. She told me they're not supposed to — not because the Glycemic Index isn't accurate, but because it might confuse people since it's so complicated. Instead, dieticians are advised to tell people with diabetes to "count carbs." Instead of learning the difference between good (high-fiber) carbs versus bad (low-fiber) carbs and cutting down on bad carbs, many diabetics are taught to cut back on all carbs. What a mistake when fiber in high-carb foods (like whole grains, legumes, fruits, and vegetables) is the single most important factor when it comes to regulating blood sugar and diabetes.

If you are concerned about diabetes, check the labels on all the food you eat for fiber content, and count fiber, not total carbs. It doesn't matter if the fiber is soluble or non-soluble (soluble and non-soluble fiber have so many similarly beneficial properties, like lowering blood cholesterol, it's not worth distinguishing between them), just make sure you're consuming at least 25 grams a day.

High fiber foods also prevent diabetes in another powerful way. The fats found in high-fiber foods such as seeds and nuts are "good" fats because they allow the cell membranes in our bodies to become more permeable, or pliable. The more permeable our cell membranes, the easier it is for insulin to bring blood sugar out of the blood and into the cell, where it belongs. These fats are found throughout foods high in fiber as well as in extra-virgin olive oil and canola oil, and they include monounsaturated fat and Omega-3 fatty acids.

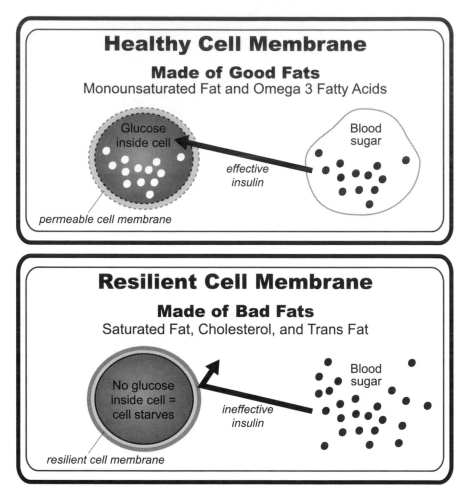

Fats in foods that don't contain fiber are the "bad" fats. Saturated fat, trans fat, and cholesterol make cell membranes more resilient, making it hard for insulin to bring glucose into the cells. Over time the cells become resistant to insulin. Saturated fat and cholesterol come primarily from animal-origin foods: eggs, meat, poultry, fish, and dairy products.

One current myth says that by eating poultry and fish in place of red meat, you can avoid these dangerous fats. This is only partly true. Poultry and fish do have significantly less saturated fat than red meat, but they all have the same amount of cholesterol. Considering the large role cholesterol plays in insulin resistance, we can't simply substitute the same amount of chicken for red meat. We need to scale way back on all meats, or cut them out altogether

Trans fats (partially hydrogenated oils) are found primarily in processed foods and restaurant food. The government now requires food manufacturers to list the grams of trans fat on labels. But ever noticed a food label claim of "0 grams trans fat" when partially hydrogenated oils appears on the ingredient list? This is because the food industry is allowed to round down. If a serving of food has less than 0.5 grams of trans fat, the manufacturer is allowed to put zero on the label. While this may seem like a negligible amount, think how small that serving size is. Most people eat two or three servings of any given food at one sitting. Lord knows I do. Also, if we are consuming many foods that each contain small amounts of partially hydrogenated oil, that is going to add up, and our cells will be the victims.

Colon Exercise

Our colon perpetually reminds us of the importance of fiber – and that's a good thing.

A bowel movement should be an easy experience. It should be fast, well lubricated, and relieving. It should never be painful or time consuming. If you are able to read literature of any kind on the pot, it's taking too long. And believe it or not, it shouldn't even be very stinky.

The colon is an involuntary muscle, meaning we can't contract it at will. You might be able to exercise your Kegel muscles anytime, but not your colon. But like any muscle tissue, if it's not exercised often, it will atrophy. When the colon atrophies, it gives us problems like Irritable Bowel Syndrome, colitis, diverticulitis, irregularity, hemorrhoids and constipation.

How do we exercise our colon? By ingesting fibrous foods of course.

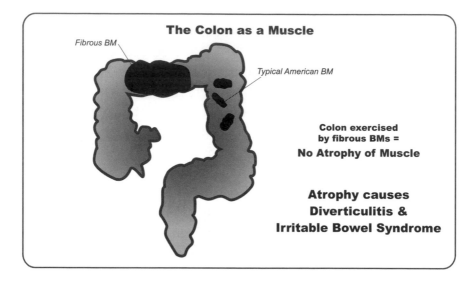

The Colon as a Muscle

Fibrous BM

Typical American BM

Colon exercised by fibrous BMs = No Atrophy of Muscle

Atrophy causes Diverticulitis & Irritable Bowel Syndrome

When we consume a high-fiber diet, our stools bulk up. (Since fiber pulls out cholesterol and bile in our bodies, the colon is lubricated well enough to handle the load.) The bigger stools push on the colon wall, making the muscle contract and push back. This makes the colon a strong muscle. It also decreases the time required for that stool to move through the colon. A shorter transit time means regularity.

Since excrement contains toxic substances, you want the least amount of exposure of those toxins to the colon wall. The bigger and more fibrous the bowel movement, the more toxins it is able to pull out of the body, thus preventing all types of cancer. Also, when bulky stools rub against the colon wall, they remove potentially toxic fatty deposits. One study showed colon cancer risk for people who ate beans, peas or lentils at least twice a week was half that of people who didn't consume these fibrous foods.[3]

Since the average American eats very little high-fiber food, most Americans' bowel movements are a series of tiny globs. Because they're small and don't push against the colon wall, they stay in there a long time. This causes bacteria to grow, producing CO_2 (as in gas and bloating) as a by-product. When the excrement does come out, all that bacteria makes things really smelly. Who would have guessed that poop doesn't have to be that stinky?

If you haven't noticed, less bulky stools also mean more straining. Over time, this results in hemorrhoids. Hemorrhoids are varicose veins in the worst place: the rectum. And believe it or not, repeated straining can cause varicose veins in the legs, especially during pregnancy (pregnant women have a higher incidence of constipation). Thankfully, I can personally attest that a high fiber diet can prevent straining, and varicose veins, even when pregnant.

And if that weren't enough, tiny stools can get stuck in the appendix. This is one of the major causes of appendicitis.

Studies have shown that people who are frequently constipated are at more than four times the risk for developing colon cancer.[4] Constipation isn't just an inconvenience; it's your body's way of telling you something needs to change, and that something is fiber. So listen up.

Leaky Gut Syndrome

According to Digestive Wellness by Elisabeth Lispki, MS, CCN, a low-fiber diet can cause dysbiosis, a precursor to Leaky Gut Syndrome. Dysbiosis means an unhealthy balance of intestinal bacteria: "bad" bacteria outnumber beneficial ones. Low-fiber diets increase stool transit time, allowing toxic by-products of digestion to concentrate and irritate the lining of the digestive tract. These toxic by-products can decrease levels of beneficial intestinal bacteria.[5]

The most common type of dysbiosis is called "putrefaction dysbiosis." It comes from a "typical American high-fat, high-animal-protein, low-fiber diet." [6] According to Lipski, research has implicated putrefaction dysbiosis with breast and colon cancer. This type of dysbiosis can be corrected by increasing high-fiber foods while decreasing meats and fats. The fiber helps to clean the colon and remove layers of debris that may contain detrimental microorganisms.

Other suspected causes of Leaky Gut Syndrome are antibiotics, steroid hormones (including oral contraceptives), antacids, and non-steroidal anti-inflammatory drugs such as aspirin and ibuprofen. High doses of antibiotics and steroid hormones are routinely given to livestock in the US today, and we consume them in conventionally raised meat and poultry, farmed fish, eggs, and dairy products. Since the proteins found in cow's milk are not completely digestible in humans, milk consumption is also believed to contribute to dysbiosis.

The scientific term for Leaky Gut Syndrome is "increased intestinal permeability." The digestive lining becomes overly porous, and bacteria, parasites, toxins, and fungi meant for removal via the gastrointestinal tract leak into the bloodstream. Along with unwanted toxins, partially undigested proteins from food also pass through the intestine, causing the body to attack not only those proteins, but the body's own tissue that is similar to these proteins. (Many cells in our body resemble specific proteins from food.)

Food intolerances to wheat, corn, soy, and milk as well as auto-immune diseases including asthma, rheumatoid arthritis, colitis, Crohn's disease, Chronic Fatigue Syndrome, Inflammatory Bowel Disease, fibromyalgia, Cystic Fibrosis, Candida, lupus, type I diabetes, and frequent headaches are all strongly associated with Leaky Gut Syndrome.

Mary took my nutrition class because she had been diagnosed with rheumatoid arthritis, a painful, debilitating auto-immune disease. Before today's medications were developed, people with this disorder were confined to wheelchairs, since it quickly deteriorates joint tissue. Mary was given chemotherapy as a treatment, which has the side effect of organ damage. Just two months after increasing high-fiber foods and removing meat and dairy from her diet, she went into remission, which meant her immune cells stopped attacking her joint tissue. Her physician was able to cut her chemotherapy treatment to one-fourth the original amount. After more than a year in remission, Mary is excited to tell everyone she knows the power of a high-fiber diet.

What we eat is just that powerful – for better or worse.

Reasons to Eat a High-Fiber Diet

- Weight loss
- Prevents and reverses type II diabetes
- Lowers cholesterol
- Regulates bile production, preventing gall stones
- Removes toxins from the body
- Prevents colon disorders and colon cancer
- Prevents hemorrhoids and varicose veins
- Establishes healthy intestinal flora
- Prevents Leaky Gut Syndrome, auto-immune disorders, and food intolerances
- Fibrous foods are loaded with nutrients.

So forget counting calories. Count fiber intake instead. Eat twenty-five to forty grams every day to lose weight, prevent or reverse diabetes, and exercise that colon.

Note of caution: If you are presently consuming a low-fiber diet, increase the amount of fiber in your food gradually over the course of a few months. For example, increase the amount of fiber you are currently consuming by 5 grams the first week, and stay at that level for three weeks. At the end of that time, increase fiber consumption by another 5 grams and remain at that level for another three weeks, until you eventually reach your goal of 35 grams of fiber. If you consume canned beans, drain the liquid and rinse the beans to remove gas. If you cook your own beans, soak them overnight (or at least 3 hours), then drain and cover with fresh water before cooking.

This will allow your digestive tract to acclimate, so you'll feel better and be less likely to lose friends in the process.

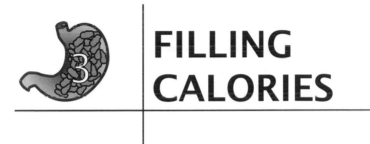

FILLING CALORIES

If you haven't noticed, fiber is filling. I mean, have you ever overeaten bean burritos?

After you've eaten something high in fiber, you feel completely full yet not stuffed. This is another key to freedom in eating: you are never hungry, nor are you uncomfortably full. Hallelujah.

Soluble fiber binds with water in the stomach and expands, leaving no space for anything else. In addition, fiber in food regulates the rate at which glucose enters the blood, so the blood sugar is stable for a long time. This also keeps us from getting hungry.

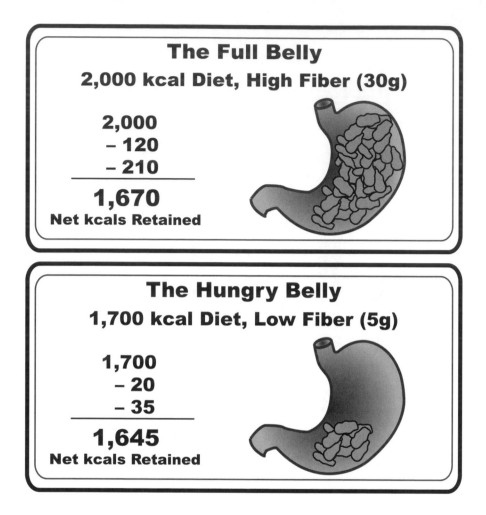

The Full Belly

2,000 kcal Diet, High Fiber (30g)

2,000
– 120
– 210
1,670
Net kcals Retained

The Hungry Belly

1,700 kcal Diet, Low Fiber (5g)

1,700
– 20
– 35
1,645
Net kcals Retained

Good Hormones

A high-fiber diet produces appetite-curbing hormones. One of these hormones is Peptide YY, or PYY. In a study cited in The New England Journal of Medicine, researchers gave this hormone to both thin and obese people. Both groups of people consumed significantly less food during this period.[1] Of course, pharmaceutical companies are trying to make a pill from PYY. But each of us would have PPY in abundance if simply we ate according to the way our bodies are designed.

Another hormone that is produced when we eat high-fiber foods is cholecystokinin, or CCK. This hormone creates a feeling of fullness that helps you stop eating when you're no longer hungry.

In one of my seminars, a student told me that when he tried to get his elderly mother to switch from white bread to wheat, she said, "I like white bread better because whole-wheat bread makes me too full, and I can't finish my sandwiches."

After I spoke to a group of parents concerned about childhood obesity, a woman came up to me and said, "You know, buying whole-grain breads and cereals is more expensive initially, but in the long run it's actually cheaper." When I asked her why, she told me that she became so full from whole-grain foods she didn't need to buy as much.

I'm telling you.

Good Fat

In addition to fiber, dietary fat also increases satiety. And unlike the 1980's, we now know that fat in food doesn't make us fat. But for those of us who are still leery of fat calories, let's imagine a little scenario: you've just come home from a hard workout and you're famished. Surprisingly, someone has rearranged your dining room while you were gone. On one end of the table you find a gigantic bowl of fresh fruit, and at the other, a similar bowl filled with avocados and assorted nuts. Now, in all honesty, which bowl are you going to naturally gravitate toward? The "high fat" bowl of avocados and nuts, of course.

But here's the deal: you will only need to eat perhaps one avocado and a handful of nuts before you're full. This is because all that fat (and protein from the nuts) is going to increase your satiety much faster than foods low in fat. If you avoided these foods because you were afraid of fat and steered yourself toward the fruit, you'd probably have to eat the entire bowl before you became remotely full.

The moral of this scenario is that no food is "fattening", but the way we eat it is. When we eat healthy high fat foods like avocados and nuts, we are apt to eat less. In fact, the Journal of Nutrition published an article stating "epidemiological studies document an inverse association between the frequency of nut consumption and BMI".[2] In other words, population groups who consume the most nuts weigh significantly less than those who rarely consume nuts.

Studies also show that people who eat nuts regularly are also less likely to develop Type II diabetes and heart disease.[3] This is because nuts (and avocados) not only contain ample fiber and other nutrients, but they are comprised mainly of healthy fat, such as monounsaturated fat and Omega-3 fatty acids. Monounsaturated fat is known for reducing LDL, or "bad" cholesterol while simultaneously boosting HDL, or "good", cholesterol levels, thereby preventing heart disease. Omega-3 fatty acids are well known for their role in blood clot prevention, so they improve circulation as well as boost immunity.

So even if you feel guilty snacking on such delicious foods as nuts, nut butters and avocados, you'll find yourself less hungry at your next meal. You'll be less likely to gain weight and develop chronic disease. They're the new "health foods".

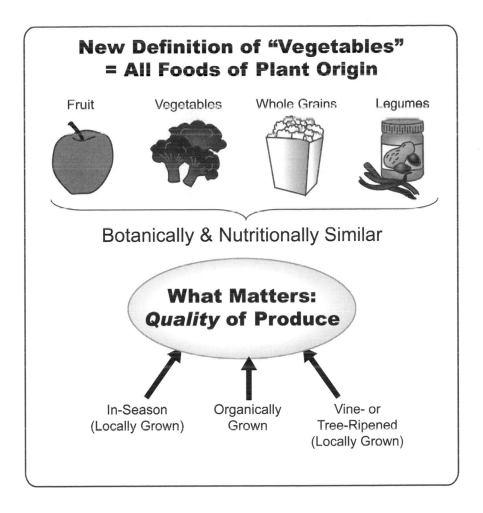

New Definition of "Vegetables"
= All Foods of Plant Origin

Fruit   Vegetables   Whole Grains   Legumes

Botanically & Nutritionally Similar

What Matters:
Quality of Produce

In-Season   Organically   Vine- or
(Locally Grown)   Grown   Tree-Ripened
                                   (Locally Grown)

Good Minerals

Another reason fibrous food makes us full is a trace mineral called chromium. Chromium has been marketed as a "weight-loss supplement." It is known for its role in preventing and reversing type II diabetes. Chromium also helps clean plaque from our arteries.

But don't run out and buy a chromium supplement: chromium works best in our bodies through food. And it's found almost exclusively in high-fiber foods.

Since most Americans do not consume enough high-fiber foods, we have artificially elevated appetites, excess arterial plaque and insulin resistance. But once we start consuming those foods, our appetites and bodies will be right on track.

Good Soil

All high-fiber foods contain chromium. But foods grown on nutrient-replete soil contain more chromium than others.

Studies show that organically grown crops have significantly higher levels of vitamins and minerals (including chromium) than commercially grown.[4] Organic foods cost more, but you receive far more nutrients for your money. And you can quit with the expensive supplements.

You are also consuming fewer toxic pesticides when you eat organically grown foods. Because there's no spraying of pesticides, organic crops need to have strong natural immunity to pests and disease, and that comes from healthy soil. Also, when pesticides are off limits, farmers use other practices to fight pests, including crop rotation, polyculture, nitrogen-fixing plants, fallow periods, crop spacing, and crop covering. All of these practices increase the nutrient density of the soil and, therefore, what's produced on it.

So please see the extra price on organic food as an investment in your health. You're getting more vitamins, minerals, and disease-fighting phytochemicals. You don't need to waste money on supplements. And I don't know about you, but I say a lower likelihood of cancer is priceless.

Nutrient Retention

Produce that is in season, locally grown, and vine/tree ripened retains more nutrients. Tomatoes at supermarkets never taste as good as the ones grown in your own backyard because they've lost nutrients along the way. Many are picked unripe, then trucked in from far away, and are often out of season.

When produce is harvested before it's ripe, the crops are not able to develop all the vitamins, antioxidants, and phytochemicals they are supposed to produce. But agriculture that's imported from great lengths has to be harvested prematurely, or those fruits and vegetables will turn to mush during travel.

Even if a crop was harvested while ripe, and was able to make it to the market before turning to sauce, the time lag between when it was picked and when it arrived at the store causes countless nutrients to be lost. And extra pesticides had to be sprayed on it if it was shipped and/or trucked for a long time.

Produce that is sold out of season has most likely been in cold storage for months, losing nutrients. Wax may have been applied to the produce in order to seal in water and keep it looking good. But the nutrients still diminish at a rapid rate. You can bet if there's wax on your apple or cucumber, it is one old piece of produce.

I have recently begun to grow a garden, and it's easier and more satisfying than I previously believed. It provides me with arugula (a spicy lettuce I add to sandwiches), lettuce and greens throughout the winter, and tomatoes, peas, and corn in the summer. We also have two fruit trees (plum and nectarine) that provide us with more fruit than we can eat throughout the summer. Fruit from your own backyard – or a neighbor's – is free, organic, fresh and nutrient-laden.

Where do you shop? I love farmer's markets and local co-ops. I also subscribe to a Community Supported Agriculture group. CSAs are organic farms that deliver weekly to nearby locations. To find a CSA near you, check out

www.localharvest.org/csa

Just put in your zip code to find a farm near you.

Nutrients and Fertility

The extra nutrients we derive from fresh, organic produce are even associated with increased fertility in humans. Eating fruits and vegetables can improve fertility in men.

Researchers from the University of Rochester compared the dietary intake of antioxidants in ten fertile and forty-eight infertile men and correlated the findings with sperm motility. Infertile men were twice as likely to have a low intake of fruits and vegetables (less than five servings per day) compared with fertile men. Men with the lowest overall intake of dietary antioxidants had lower sperm motility than men with higher intakes.[5]

The book, *The Fertility Diet,* reveals that women who eat more plant-based foods are more fertile than women who eat diets higher in animal-derived protein.[6]

Antioxidants derived from food fight free radicals. Free radicals destroy cells and cell DNA. Therefore, eating a diet high in antioxidants will help keep sperm cells and other reproductive tissue healthy. So if you're concerned about fertility, invest your money in a plant-based diet. Doesn't that sound better than medical treatments?

NUTRITIOUS CALORIES

"Health food" isn't just sprouts and spinach, thank goodness. Nutritionally speaking, legumes (beans, lentils, peas, seeds, nuts, and nut butters) are comparable with vegetables. Botanically, they are very similar. Legumes are usually the "seed" that leads to a vegetable, so they're full of the nutrients the vegetable will eventually contain.

If I were the Food Dictator (and how I wish I were), I would put legumes in the category of vegetables. Imagine how many more people would eat their "vegetables", or how few parents would worry about their children's diet. In fact, without beans my 5-year-old daughter would have starved long ago. How good to know almonds don't just help us lose weight - they nourish us.

Legumes often have more folic acid than many fruits and vegetables. Ounce per ounce, they are higher in fiber and many other nutrients. Legumes are usually dried; therefore, their nutrients are less likely to perish over time than with fresh fruit and vegetables. The only nutrient that fruits and vegetables have and legumes lack is vitamin C.

Now, you may not want to tell your kids that peanut butter, pistachios, and sunflower seeds are health foods. But isn't it great that there are foods you like that will help you lose weight and live naturally?

Food Is Medicine

Years ago in graduate school, my professor taught us, "Food is medicine". Today I believe that statement more than ever. Healthy, high-fiber foods are excellent preventive medicine. Those who don't eat these foods end up paying later for other types of medicine or surgery. There is no substitute for good nutrition.

Some supposed substitutes are vitamin and mineral supplements. But if these things really worked, Americans would be the healthiest people on earth. And well, we're not.

People are often shocked to hear I don't promote supplements. As a vegetarian, I do need to make sure I'm getting sufficient vitamin B12 in my diet, but that's fortified in my soymilk and most cereals. So no, I don't take one vitamin or mineral supplement - and neither should you.

Nutrients (such as vitamins and minerals) compete with one another for carriers, enzymes, and absorption in the body. Because nutrients compete, too much of some – as from supplements – can cause the depletion of others. By contrast, the multiple nutrients found naturally in food provide a healthy "check and balance" system that helps each one to be effective in our bodies. Food-derived nutrients help keep any one nutrient from being over-absorbed, which could cause toxicity. This is commonly referred to as the "synergistic effects of food", meaning that nutrients found in food work harmoniously, as opposed to supplements.

I know this may sound old-fashioned, but there's no

better place to find nutrients than in food. With supplements (whether it's a multivitamin or a single or complex supplement, like calcium with magnesium), there's no natural check and balance. You are self-medicating with high levels of certain nutrients, which can lower other nutrient stores in your body.

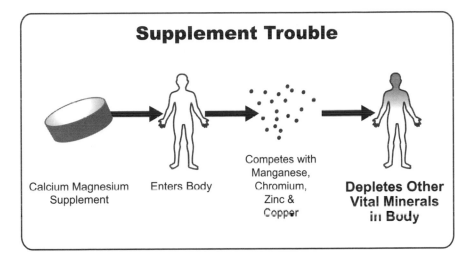

Supplement Trouble

Calcium Magnesium Supplement

Enters Body

Competes with Manganese, Chromium, Zinc & Copper

Depletes Other Vital Minerals in Body

For example, calcium is a commonly taken supplement. But since nutrients compete for absorption and retention in the body, minerals like zinc, copper, and magnesium can become depleted.[1] Ironically, we need all these minerals to prevent bone loss. In fact, one study found elderly women taking calcium were no less likely to lose bone mass, but more likely to develop heart disease than those taking a placebo (dummy pill).[2] The outcome was likely due to the depletion of minerals such as copper, chromium and manganese caused by taking calcium supplements.

Contrary to popular belief, multivitamins do not contain all the nutrients we need to live. You may get certain nutrients, but by doing so in an artificial manner you are likely to develop deficiencies in other areas.

Studies have found that some nutrients become dangerous when consumed in supplemental form. For instance, antioxidants (beta-carotene, vitamins C and E, selenium, copper, and magnesium, to name a few) can cause the same oxidative damage as free radicals—the very thing we want antioxidants to protect us from—when consumed outside food.[3]

So supplements may actually play are role in causing cancer, rather than preventing it. Question: why are we paying for this?

Modern-Day Snake Oil

Have you ever seen a movie or read a book set in early America where there's a "snake oil" salesman? Usually he's standing on a literal soapbox, pitching his claim that his oil is a cure-all. And of course, people are lining up to buy it.

Today we look back and think how silly our great-grandparents were to believe this con artist. But we are being conned today into taking vitamin/mineral supplements. And it's a multi-billion-dollar con game.

A report by Trevor Marshall, PhD, professor at Australia's Murdoch University School of Biological Medicine and Biotechnology states, "Low blood levels of vitamin D have long been associated with disease, and the assumption has been that vitamin D supplements may protect against disease. However, this *new research demonstrates that ingested vitamin D is immunosuppressive… Supplementation may make the disease worse*" (emphasis mine).[4]

The following is an excerpt from Stanford University's Nutrition Studies Department:

A long history of epidemiological studies has suggested that dietary (food-derived) antioxidants are associated with prevention of heart disease.

However, several recent large clinical trials using high doses of antioxidant supplements, such as vitamin E, beta carotene, and vitamin C, have yielded disappointing and controversial results. Despite these null findings, the use of antioxidant supplements in the U.S. continues to grow.[5]

Why, despite "null findings", does supplement use continue to grow? Let's just say snake oil has a great sales history.

One of the most surprising places we find snake oil promoted is in our doctor's office. As you may know, physicians are well versed in treating disease with drugs and surgery, but not nutrition (most medical schools do not require a nutrition class, and for those that do, the information covered is extremely basic). So taking nutrition advice from a medical doctor is akin to asking your local dry cleaner for tips on car maintenance. The little information doctors do receive on nutrients tends to be in the form of brochures from supplement companies, citing industry-sponsored studies, giving them a very one-sided view of supplements.

This helps explain a recent experience I had with my own doctor. After finding I had low iron levels (most women have "low", or "borderline" iron levels throughout their menstruating years due to monthly blood loss), he prescribed that I take not one, not two, but three iron supplements a day. In addition, he prescribed taking those supplements along with a vitamin C pill, since vitamin C is known to help in iron absorption. In other words, my doctor wanted me to take six supplements a day.

But here's what he didn't know: one of the reasons it is believed women commonly outlive men is because the relatively "low" iron status throughout their reproductive years protects them against aging. Iron is such a powerful pro-oxidant, it is notorious for free radical damage, causing liver, heart and arterial damage. Researchers believe the higher levels of iron found in most men causes oxidation of LDL cholesterol, leading to arteriosclerosis. Since current iron standards are based on iron levels in men, you might see those standards drop in the near future.

Vitamin C is also a known pro-oxidant in supplement form. And if that weren't enough, vitamin C's role in iron absorption is found primarily in food, not pills.

So if I weren't the ever-vigilant supplement skeptic that I am, I would follow my doctor's advice, creating levels of free radicals that could easily result in cancer cells or excess arterial plaque, with no outweighing benefits.

This isn't to say we shouldn't ever take the advice of physicians, but let's definitely do our research – especially on areas outside their speciality.

Anti–Aging Eating

Nutritious foods prevent many of the illnesses we associate with aging. Most of us assume that as we age we will become arthritic and impotent, develop cataracts or macular degeneration (blindness), lose mental acuity, and develop osteoporosis to some degree. Yet nutrients can play an enormous role in preventing these disorders. People who eat a nutrient-laden diet are much less likely to have such problems.

You probably know one or more elderly people who are sharp as a tack and are in kick-ass shape. You might even know there are elderly athletes, competing in the Senior Olympics into their late-90's. Why do some seniors age gracefully, without developing the disorders we associate with growing old? Exercise plays a major role in strengthening the heart and clearing our arteries, but so does a high fiber diet, because it increases oxygen flow to the heart, brain and other organs. Even those of us who aren't athletic can keep living naturally thin into our senior years.

In his book, *Healthy at 100*, author John Robbins examines four remote people groups (two in the Near East, one in South America, and the Okinawans in Japan) who were studied in great detail within the last 40 years, and noted for their longevity. These folks shocked researchers since not only did a high percentage live to be centenarians (100+ years old), but they lived incredibly healthy, mobile lives often well into their 90's. Investigators found almost no cancer, dementia, arthritis, diabetes, or signs of heart disease at all. And perhaps best of all, people took very little time to die, as opposed to living with chronic disease for decades.

So besides physical activity, what do these populations have in common? Of course, their diets were free from processed foods since they lived in remote areas. What did they eat? Mostly plant foods. Each group consumed 90% or more of their calories from fruit, vegetables, grains and legumes. In addition, you can bet their produce was fresh since imported foods didn't exist. These people ate plant foods that were organic, locally-grown, and in season. This kind of diet could not possibly contain more age-fighting antioxidants: it is a nutritionist's dream... and a real life reminder to the rest of us that what we eat determines the way we age.

Americans are living to longer ages than ever before (due primarily to drugs and medical technology), but we're also taking longer to die. We spend many of our "golden years" in pain, often completely dependent upon others to care for us.

So in case you don't read *Healthy at 100* for yourself, please remember this: we are not destined to suffer chronic disease in a care facility in our senior years. We have the power to prevent disease and aging, but the time to use this power isn't when we've been diagnosed with an illness – it's right now.

Arthritis

There are two main kinds of arthritis, osteoarthritis and rheumatoid, and both are linked with nutrition. Omega-3 fatty acids (from plant foods such as flaxseed and oil, nuts and seeds, avocados, olive and canola oils, to name a few) are renowned for preventing osteoarthritis. This precious nutrient can even help arthritic people get rid of their pain.

Years ago I had an elderly neighbor who had this type of arthritis in her knees to such a degree that she could hardly walk. In fact, I made her acquaintance precisely because she could only walk to my house – two houses away – where her dog would poop on my lawn. As we got to know each other, I mentioned the power of Omega-3 fat from plants in reversing arthritis. I asked if I could buy her a cereal containing flaxseed and soy milk, both of which contain lots of Omega-3 fatty acids. She agreed. One week later, this "arthritic" old woman was walking to the store, a half-mile away, to buy these things herself. She also walked her dog further down the block. Talk about a win-win situation.

Omega-3 isn't the only compound in plant foods that fights arthritis. Phytochemicals is a term for the myriad beneficial compounds found in plant foods. Most phytochemicals have powerful antioxidant properties. Many prevent joint inflammation.

Boron, a trace mineral found in plant foods, is also important in fighting arthritis. Conversely, the protein found in dairy products, as well as the saturated fat and cholesterol from animal-origin foods, is known to cause or exacerbate rheumatoid and osteoarthritis.

Getting all the nutrients we need from food prevents chronic disease from colon disorders to cancer, arthritis to diabetes. And of course, weight loss isn't a bad side effect.

THE TRUTH
ABOUT
SUGAR AND STARCH

By now maybe you're convinced that you need to eat more fruits and vegetables. You may be wondering what options you have. The answer may surprise you.

If you've been trying to add more vegetables to your diet, you may be consuming more tomatoes, cucumbers, zucchini, squash, eggplant, avocados, and corn. But guess what? These aren't really vegetables; technically they're fruit or grains. There are actually very few real vegetables. Most are leafy greens, broccoli, and root vegetables such as potatoes and carrots.

The potato *is* a vegetable, but it's gotten a bad rap for being a "starch." Why? Partly because most Americans add less-than-healthy toppings to their potatoes, like butter, cheese, bacon, and sour cream.

The other thing we do to a potato is peel the poor thing. Yet most of the fiber and other nutrients are in the skin. Without the skin, a potato still has some fiber (about two grams). But with its peel, an average potato contains five grams of fiber. Let's get this straight: an unpeeled potato is a fiber bomb.

Potatoes do contain starch, but we need starch in order to live. And the rate of that starch's entry into the bloodstream as blood sugar will be slower with the skin, verses without, making us less likely to develop diabetes. We'll also be negating more calories, increasing our metabolism, consuming more chromium and getting fuller, if we eat potatoes skin and all.

So remember: potatoes are vegetables. Enjoy them guilt-free.

Dried fruit is another good way to get the nutrients you need. One common objection to eating dried fruit is the amount of sugar it contains. Ounce per ounce, dried fruit does contain more sugar than fresh since it is more concentrated. And sugar is often added as a natural preservative. But don't let that stop you from eating a ridiculous amount of dried fruit. We need the fiber punch these foods have, as well as the nutrients. Dried fruit is especially strategic since you can stash it anywhere: your car, desk, purse, and gym locker. And it won't go bad because it's already dried.

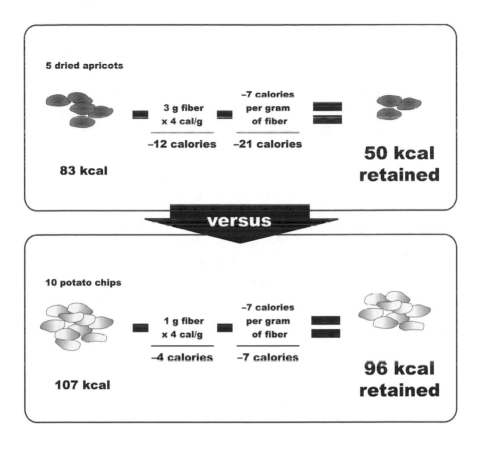

Of course, fresh fruit is full of fiber and nutrients and should be eaten with abandon. But just try carrying around a bag of apples with you all day.

The Scoop on Sugar

If you're still hung up about all that sugar, remember that fiber, when found in the same foods as starch and sugar, slows the rate of the other carbohydrates' absorption into the blood. If you are consuming foods high in fiber, you can prevent diabetes and eat freely no matter how much sugar or starch is in those foods.

However, if a large percentage of your diet is comprised of sweets, you're eating too many empty calories. Surprise. But if you are consuming a diet of high-fiber foods and have a little chocolate now and then, that's fine. Or if you're eating a healthy cereal that's high in fiber, don't worry about the sugar content. What is important is all those other nutrients you are getting.

Our focus shouldn't be on staying away from sugar but on trying to get as many healthy foods as possible into our diet. Sugar doesn't make us fat or give us diabetes; nutrient-poor foods do. You could eat a sugar-free diet and eat really horribly. Or you could eat a nutrient-rich diet with some sugar. Sometimes a spoonful (not truckload) of sugar helps the medicine go down.

Neither should we blame sugar for hyperactivity in children. When we realize that those sweets they're consuming also contain artificial colors and flavors, the real culprit is obvious. Studies show that when children diagnosed with ADD have artificial colors and flavors removed from their diet, they improve significantly. These additives, known as "excitotoxins," overstimulate nervous cells and often destroy nerve tissue.[1]

Fruit and Vegetable Fiber Content

So, how many grams of fiber do fruits and veggies contain? I'll give a more exhaustive list in the appendix, but here are a few for inspiration.

Fruit:

Medium apple with peel: 4–5 grams

Medium orange: 4 grams

Three small apricots: 6 grams

Pear with peel: 5 grams

Avocado: 8 grams

1 cup dates: 13 grams

10 figs: 18 grams

1 cup raspberries: 8 grams

Vegetables:

1 artichoke: 6.5 grams

2/3 cup artichoke hearts: 6 grams

1 cup cooked broccoli: 5 grams

Dried Fruit:

1 cup sun-dried tomatoes: 7 grams

1 cup raisins: 5 grams

10 dried plums: 6 grams

10 dried peaches: 11 grams

6 | BEANS ARE THE NEW MEAT

Nuts, nut butters, seeds, lentils, and peas are all high in fiber and protein. But legumes (like beans) are the protein powerhouses of the plant-origin foods. These are the best foods to replace meat because they make us full. But unlike meat (chicken, turkey, fish, and pork), beans have fiber. Meat "rots" in the digestive tract, while beans are in and out in less than half a day.

Legumes also have the best kind of protein. Most Americans consume twice the amount of protein they need (mainly from animal-origin foods), and it's causing hypertension, diabetes, cancer, kidney stones, and osteoporosis.

Protein–Deficiency Myths

Believe it or not, protein is the most difficult of all nutrients to become deficient in. Studies worldwide, including in extremely poor countries, have found that the majority of protein deficiency exists only where people have a severe calorie shortage; i.e., famine. This is called "Protein-Calorie Malnutrition", meaning that protein deficiency only happens with an overall calorie deficit.[1]

All natural (as opposed to processed, man-made) food contains protein. It's estimated most people only need between forty and sixty grams of protein a day. Only nine of the 22 amino acids in protein are essential. Besides soybeans, most plant-origin foods do not contain all nine of these essential amino acids. But when we are eating a varied diet, we are bound to consume them all. And they don't all need to be consumed at one meal, or even in one day, but over the course of a week or so.

For instance, if you ate only bread for a whole week, you might develop an amino acid or protein deficiency. But if sometime during that week you added peanut butter to your bread, you would have all nine essential amino acids. If you ate only corn all week, you could develop an amino-acid deficiency. But if you added some beans at a meal or two, there goes your problem. In other words, to develop a protein deficiency, you'd have to be pretty nuts (no pun intended).

Another deficiency myth says that if you don't eat meat you won't get enough B vitamins. Actually, there's only one B vitamin you need to be concerned about: B12. This vitamin is not found in any plant foods, and thus has been a long-standing argument for meat consumption. However, the liver can store this vitamin for up to five years. Healthy intestinal flora, or "good bacteria" are also involved in producing B12. So B12 deficiency is rare (except among elderly people unable to produce a certain enzyme necessary for B12 absorption).

B12 is produced by bacteria. That's right: bacteria. These microbes live in soil (aside from your intestines), and when livestock eat grass, they consume soil residue that contains the microbial-produced B12 vitamin. That's how B12 gets into animal foods.

One of my professors once told a story about an Indian family who developed a B12 deficiency after moving to the U.S. The family ate a strict vegan, or plant-based, diet. Apparently in Indian markets, the produce isn't washed as well as in American supermarkets, and they consumed plenty of B12 through the soil residue in their food before their move. While I don't propose we all eat unwashed produce, since soil can harbor pathogens like E.Coli, I think it's an interesting illustration of where B12 really comes from.

Most soy milks and many cereals are B12 fortified, so we don't have to eat meat – or soil – if we don't want to.

The Iron Deficiency Myth

Another common myth is that meat is the best source of iron, since the iron in meat (called "heme" iron) is more readily absorbed. As we are discover the role excess iron plays in cancer, arteriosclerosis and premature aging, highly absorbable iron becomes less attractive to researchers. In addition, the most commonly known genetic disorder in humans is called hemochromatosis. People suffering from this disorder are unable to rid excess iron at healthy levels, and therefore iron accumulates, increasing rates of heart disease and liver cancer.

Plant foods, including vegetables, whole grains and legumes contain what's known as non-heme iron. Although non-heme iron has traditionally been recognized as inferior to heme iron from meat, we are now finding the truth is just the opposite. With non-heme iron, our body only absorbs what it needs. When our iron levels are low, we absorb more iron from vegetable sources, and when our iron levels are high we absorb less iron. Thus, non-heme iron is much less likely to contribute to free radical formation and disease.

Meat, Osteoporosis, and Kidney Stones

Vegetarians have denser bones at older ages than meat-eating folk because animal protein creates uric and sulfuric acid, and all that acid needs to be neutralized.[2] Our bodies respond by leaching out calcium from the bones as a buffer. Unfortunately, after the calcium does its work, it doesn't return to the bones, but lands either in the toilet or stockpiles in the kidneys, creating kidney stones.

In other words, bone calcium comprises part of that "mineral buildup" in our toilet bowl. Next time you clean your toilet, you might want to keep this in mind. In addition to soda and processed foods, high consumption of animal protein is a major cause for osteoporosis in our society.

This explains a bunch when you're a nutritionist. Like my forty-something nutrition student who was on a low-carb (high protein) diet for three years, and spent two years passing one kidney stone after another. Once she took my class and got off this diet, her kidney stones stopped. I had another student who had kidney stones at the age of twenty-five. He was a body builder, and he consumed an excessive amount of protein.

The American Journal of Kidney Disease found that people on the maintenance phase of the Atkins diet lost calcium in urine at rates 55 percent higher than normal.[3] But you don't have to be on an extreme diet to lose bone density. The typical American diet is twice as high in protein as it should be. Damage to our bones is just the start of the problems caused by the excess protein.

Meats and Hormones

Hormone levels in meat are a growing concern.[4] There are more hormones used than ever before, and measurable levels are routinely present in the animals' muscle, fat, livers, kidneys, and other organs we consume. These are steroid hormones that get the animals to grow faster so they are ready for market sooner. Steroid hormones are involved in cell reproduction and growth, and they seem to be altering our own bodies' steroid levels (sex, or growth hormones), which is making us fat, giving us higher rates of cancer, lowering the age of puberty in children, and interfering with our fertility.

A study in the scientific journal Human Reproduction found that a pregnant woman's meat consumption can reduce her future son's sperm count. Researchers at the University of Rochester analyzed the relationship between various sperm parameters of 387 men and the eating habits of their mothers. The more beef a mother consumed, the lower her son's sperm concentration. Sperm count was 24 percent higher in men whose mothers consumed less beef.[5]

Have you noticed there's more infertility problems today than just a few decades ago? I mean, when we saw twins years ago, no one ever thought their parents took fertility drugs. Today it's assumed. That's because the hormones in our diet have increased. Hormones and hormone-mimicking compounds, like antibiotics given to livestock, play an enormous role in fertility. Steroid hormones (like estrogen or testosterone) drive the reproductive system. If our steroid hormones are out of whack, it makes sense that we can't get pregnant.

Even "grass-fed," "free-range," and "organic" meats can affect your hormone levels. All animals produce endogenous (their own internal) steroid hormones. Even organically raised livestock will produce natural steroid hormones. Also, many animals are given antibiotics to make them grow bigger faster. The hormones and antibiotics in our meat have the same endocrine-mimicking effects, in both the body of the animal and our own bodies.

Meats and Toxins

Toxic substances concentrate at higher levels as we go up the food chain. This is why we're told by the Environmental Protection Agency to stay away from "the big fish," especially shark and swordfish. Think about shark and swordfish – fish don't get any bigger than that. These fish are on the absolute top of the seafood chain. As we go down the food chain to anchovies, we find much lower levels of mercury and other toxins. We are never told to stay away from seaweed, even though it lives in the same mercury-infested waters, because seaweed is a plant, and plants are at the very safe bottom of the food chain.

All toxins have endocrine-mimicking effects in humans. They affect our steroid hormones the same way antibiotics and outside hormones do. Toxins also have the added danger of producing free radicals in our bodies, which lead to cancer and chronic disease.

When we eat meat, you could say we are getting lots of toxins, including mercury, pesticides, polychloronated biphenals (PCBs), dioxin, arsenic, perchlorate, etc. We are ingesting these chemicals mainly through animal-origin foods.

What about the Omega-3 fatty acids in fish? Fish is the only food of animal origin that naturally contains a significant amount of this beneficial fat. But fish is high on the food chain. As for Omega-3 fortified eggs, you might be interested to know the chickens are fed flaxseed to boost the Omega-3 levels. Flaxseed, flaxseed oil and many other whole plant foods are loaded with Omega-3 fatty acids. The fattier ones (like avocados, olives, extra-virgin olive oil, canola oil, nuts, and seeds) have more, but low-fat beans, lentils, peas, whole grains, and vegetables are chock full of them. By bypassing eggs and consuming more foods rich in Omega-3 (like flaxseed), you can avoid the toxins and cholesterol in eggs.

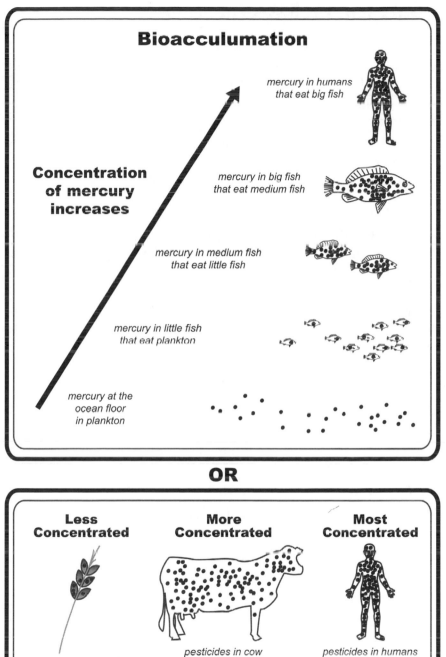

Bioacculumation

Concentration of mercury increases

mercury in humans that eat big fish

mercury in big fish that eat medium fish

mercury in medium fish that eat little fish

mercury in little fish that eat plankton

mercury at the ocean floor in plankton

OR

Less Concentrated	More Concentrated	Most Concentrated
pesticides on grain	pesticides in cow meat and milk	pesticides in humans that eat meat and milk

Meats and Heterocyclic Amines

Heterocyclic amines, or HCAs, are known carcinogens (cancer-causing compounds). They are produced when meats are cooked at high temperatures. HCAs are created when the amino acids in the meat combine with another amino acid (creatine), which is found in muscle tissue. This is true no matter how lean the meat is, even if it's fish or poultry, since HCAs are derived solely from the protein. This isn't an issue with plant-based proteins, as they contain no creatine.

Studies show that higher rates of stomach, colorectal, pancreatic, and breast cancer are associated with frequent meat consumption.[6] HCAs are particularly high in meats that are charred, broiled, well done, fried, or barbequed.

So if you want to consume a bit of meat, eat responsibly. Here are some guidelines from the National Cancer Institute:

A study conducted by researchers showed a threefold increase in the content of HCAs when the cooking temperature was increased from 200° to 250°C (392° to 482°F). Oven roasting and baking are done at lower temperatures, so lower levels of HCAs are likely to form; however, gravy made from meat drippings contains substantial amounts of HCAs. Stewing, boiling, or poaching are done at or below 100°C (212°F); cooking at this low temperature creates negligible amounts of the chemicals. Foods cooked a long time ("well done" instead of "medium") will form slightly more of the chemicals.

Meats that are partially cooked in the microwave before cooking by other methods have lower levels of HCAs. Studies have shown that microwaving meat prior to cooking helps decrease mutagens by removing the precursors. Meats that were microwaved for two minutes prior to cooking had a 90 percent decrease in HCA content. If the liquid that forms during microwaving is poured off before further cooking, the final quantity of HCAs is reduced.

Nitrates

Nitrates are preservatives, added to "cure" meat and keep its color. Nitrates and nitrite compounds are known carcinogens. The following foods contain nitrates: bacon, ham, sausage, hot dogs, and luncheon meats (even poultry).

In ages past, meats were preserved with salt, as in salted pork. Today it's nitrates. Either way, you don't want to imagine how meat would look – or smell – without preservatives. Let's just say ham wouldn't exactly be pink.

Meats and Homocysteine

Animal protein is loaded with methionine. Too much of this amino acid causes it to convert to a dangerous compound known as homocysteine. Homocysteine is connected to heart disease, stroke, hypertension, dementia and Alzheimer's, impotence, cancer, diabetes, arthritis, and osteoporosis. Homocysteine acts like a free radical in the body, damaging arterial linings and thereby creating plaque. Plaque slows down oxygen circulation, ultimately to the death of cells and tissue. The more oxygen to our tissues, the healthier we are. The more oxygen to our brain, the more alert we are.

Plant protein supplies methionine, but not at dangerous levels as with animal protein. Legumes, grains, fruit and vegetables are the best source of folic acid, a well-known natural antagonist to homocysteine.

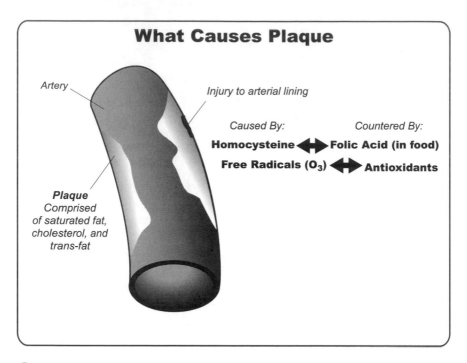

What Causes Plaque

Artery

Injury to arterial lining

Caused By: Countered By:

Homocysteine ↔ **Folic Acid (in food)**

Free Radicals (O₃) ↔ **Antioxidants**

Plaque
Comprised
of saturated fat,
cholesterol, and
trans-fat

Oxygen

Speaking of brain-energy, did you know the casinos in Las Vegas release extra oxygen into the air to keep people from getting tired? Imagine if you treated your brain cells to more oxygen by your diet. You'd become a party animal. And that's what better circulation from less plaque gives us: more energy from more oxygen.

An interesting anecdote for the power of oxygen: my husband was a shoe-in for male-pattern baldness. His dad, his mom's dad, and his dad's dad were all early baldies. I knew when I married him he stood almost no chance of keeping his hairline. Yet I developed a theory, based on lots of observation, that healthy men tended to keep their hair longer due to improved circulation bringing more oxygen to the hair follicles. Well, my husband eats a plant-based diet, like I do, and his hairline hasn't budged as he is approaching 40. Needless to say, I thought he'd look way different when I married him 15 years ago. Oxygen rocks.

Meat and Cancer

Studies show a relationship between high meat consumption and cancer risk. A study published in the International Journal of Cancer evaluated the role of dietary nutrients and the risk of endometrial cancer among 1,204 newly diagnosed endometrial cancer patients and 1,212 women without cancer in China. Results showed that those who consumed the most animal products had nearly four times the risk of cancer compared with those whose diets were derived primarily from plant sources.[7]

The American Journal of Clinical Nutrition published a study revealing a strong association between high animal protein intakes with a significantly increased risk of cancer. Participants who ate the most plant-based protein had the lowest risk indicators for cancer, and conversely, those who consumed the most animal protein had the highest levels of cancer risk indicators.[8]

Another study evaluated the relationship between meat consumption and risk of breast cancer among 24,697 postmenopausal Danish women. This nested study looked at 378 women who developed breast cancer and matched them to controls who did not develop breast cancer. A higher intake of meat (red meat, poultry, fish, and processed meat) was associated with a significantly higher breast cancer incidence rate. Every 25 gram increase in consumption of total meat, red meat, and processed meat led to a 9, 15, and 23 percent increase in risk of breast cancer, respectively.[9]

A study from the Harvard School of Public Health also found that meat—including chicken—intake is associated with an increased risk of bladder cancer. A data analysis of 47,422 men from the Health Professionals Follow-Up Study and 88,471 women from the Nurse's Health Study showed that individuals who ate more than five servings of chicken without skin each week had a 52 percent increase in bladder cancer risk compared with those who ate none. Researchers hypothesize that nitrosamines, heterocyclic amines, or both may play a role.[10]

Or, it just might be the animal protein itself that causes cancer. In the book, *The China Study*, researcher Dr. T. Colin Campbell shows that rats fed a high animal protein diet are significantly more likely to develop cancer than those consuming low amounts of animal protein. This was true even when the low-protein rats were exposed to very high levels of carcinogens, and vice-versa. These findings were also documented in human populations: Chinese people consuming the most animal protein had the highest incidence of cancer when compared with those who ate the least.[11]

I remember learning in college that cancer cells are constantly springing up in our bodies. Shocking, isn't it? Free radicals (often created from toxins) are affecting cell DNA all the time. But our body's immune system thwarts the majority of those new cancer cells.

Even more shocking is that by the time we discover that we have cancer, it has been around for a long time. After the original cancer cell is developed, that cell has to reproduce millions of times to become diagnosable. Yet it takes just three months, on average, for that first cell to double, six months to have four, and one year for sixteen. After twenty doublings, that cancer cell will grow to one million cells, which is the tiniest lump a woman can feel in her breast.

It can take between eight and twelve years for a cancer to be clinically diagnosed. Somewhere along that timeline, the cancer often stops growing, usually suppressed by the immune system's tight genetic control.

So, if cancer cells reproduce so slowly, and the immune system has so much time to fight those cells, then why so much cancer? And why so much cancer today than ever before?

Growth hormones speed up replication of all cells,

including cancer cells. If a growth hormone gets hold of a cancer cell, it doubles faster, giving the body less time to fight it. Growth hormones and antibiotics (most of which are illegal in European countries) are fed to livestock in the US to produce more meat and milk, faster and cheaper. When they are passed on to us, our cancer risk rises.

Meg's Story

One of the most amazing individuals I have come to know throughout my nutrition career is Meg Wolff. Meg spent decades of her life fighting cancer, and now, another decade later, she's still celebrating her cancer-free status. To look at Meg, who is in her early 50's, you would never know. She is slender, attractive, and looks healthier than most people in her age category. Look closer though, and Meg will show you she is missing a leg and a breast.

Meg was first diagnosed with bone cancer in her early 30's, which led to the amputation of her leg. Years later she was found to have breast cancer that spread into many lymph nodes. After many rounds of chemotherapy and life-draining drug treatments, Meg was a walking skeleton, barely able to eat or take care of herself. Her doctor told her to "make her peace with God."

Finally, Meg decided to try changing her diet. She tried a macrobiotic diet, which consists almost entirely of plant foods: vegetables, whole grains and legumes. It was this "crazy diet" – devoid of meat, eggs, and dairy products – that gave Meg back her life. Today she dedicates her life to sharing her story with the ever-increasing number of people facing cancer. She has written two books, keeps an updated website and blog, and gives seminars to groups throughout New England. In her journey, Meg has met a surprising number of people who share a remarkably similar story to hers: a plant-based diet fights cancer.

Vegetarians

Even if you don't cut meat out of your diet altogether, you can certainly cut back. Most nutritionists have been recommending smaller servings of meat for years. Traditional cultures, especially Indian and Asian, eat lots of grains, legumes, and vegetables. If meat is in their dishes, it's more of a flavoring agent than anything else. In contrast, typical American fare has meat at the center of the plate, surrounded by a wee bit of vegetables and grains.

"Vegetarian"

Even though I am not a proponent of meat consumption, I don't use titles like "vegan" and "vegetarian." I don't like being labeled as anything. Labels are misleading (even nutrition labels on food). And sometimes they lead to annoying questions like, "What do you eat at a barbecue?" or "Don't you get tired of eating just vegetables?"

Many assumptions come with the title "vegetarian." One is that vegetarians and vegans actually eat vegetables.

It's possible to be a vegetarian and yet eat very poorly. Many people who don't eat meat also eat lots of processed foods, such as white bread, white rice and pre-made foods.

I know people who eat meat in small amounts. Some eat more fruit, vegetables, whole grains, and legumes than some vegetarians. You see how this can be confusing.

So instead of going by labels, maybe we should just be more transparent: "Hi, I'm Jenny and I eat high-fiber foods 70% of the time, but I'm working towards 80%."

Chocolate

One of my favorite foods comes from a legume: chocolate. Most of us have heard all our lives not to eat chocolate because it supposedly makes people fat, contributes toward acne, and is full of sugar. Yet recent studies are showing that chocolate is actually good for us. Dark chocolate, since it's not diluted with milk, contains antioxidants and fiber. These are similar benefits we find in tea, coffee, and wine. Compounds derived from plants whether it's beans in coffee and chocolate, leaves in tea, or grapes in wine — are healthy in moderation. Plant sources are where we find fiber, although beverages such as coffee, tea, and wine contain very little. Dark chocolate has about two grams of fiber per ounce. Talk about Free to Eat!

Legumes

How much fiber do we find in legumes? A longer list is found in the appendix, but here's some immediate gratification for you.

Beans/Lentils/Peas (cooked)

1 cup limas: 12 g

1 cup pintos: 14 g

1 cup garbanzos: 8 g

1 cup kidney beans: 16 g

1 cup split pea soup: 5–7 g

Nuts/Seeds/Nut butters

1 cup almonds: 14 g

1 cup pistachios: 14 g

1 cup pumpkin seeds: 15 g

2 tablespoons natural peanut butter: 3 g

2 tablespoons almond butter: 4 g

½ cup hummus: 6

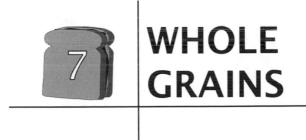

WHOLE GRAINS

We hear a lot these days about eating "whole grains" and avoiding "processed foods." Why all the fuss? It's just the difference between "living" and being abundantly alive.

Both wheat and rice, in their natural state, are comprised of three compounds: bran, germ, and endosperm. Fiber (and myriad other nutrients) are found primarily in bran and germ. Endosperm is mostly starch, with comparably few nutrients.

When we eat whole-wheat products or brown rice, we're consuming all three, allowing the fiber to regulate our blood sugar as our body metabolizes the starch. This prevents us from developing diabetes. It also allows us to become full, so we are less likely to overeat.

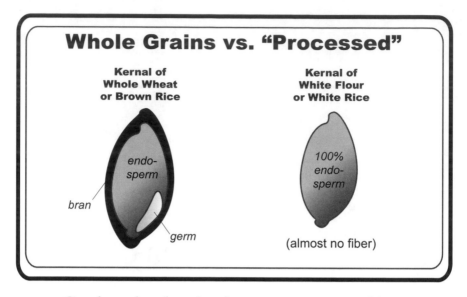

On the other hand, when we consume white rice or enriched (white) flour, we are only consuming the endosperm. That means the bran and germ got dumped. Not only are we receiving fewer nutrients and fiber, we don't get nearly as full, nor are we fighting diabetes or other disease. Grains such as wheat and rice should be eaten whole, and our bodies were designed to eat lots of them.

I hope this explains why many of us experience hunger an hour after eating Chinese food. Change that white rice to brown and just see what happens – you'll be full for a good three hours. I won't even go to an Asian restaurant that doesn't serve brown rice, since I've come to realize it's not worth the money when my hunger comes back so quickly.

So forget about adding wheat germ or bran to your cereal and smoothies. You can eat whole grains that contain germ and bran naturally by consuming whole grain products and brown rice.

Good and Bad Carbohydrates

Why are some carbohydrates termed "bad" and others "good"? Bad carbs are the refined, processed version of the high-fiber, natural food. Some diet "experts" in the past have said that carrots, potatoes, beans, and grains are bad based solely on their carb content, claiming that if you take all or almost all carbs out of your diet, you will lose weight. And it's true. You'd lose weight if you took any food group out of your diet. But it won't last long because it's not realistic.

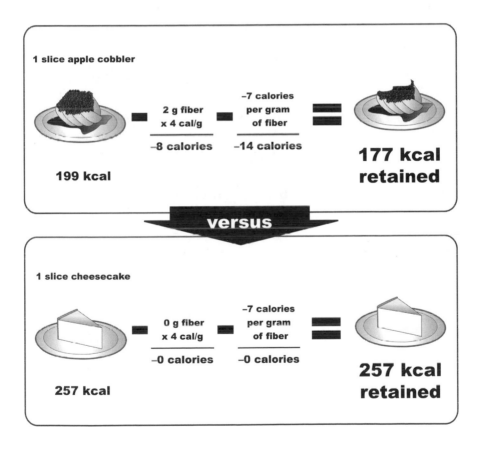

1 slice apple cobbler

199 kcal — 2 g fiber x 4 cal/g / −8 calories — −7 calories per gram of fiber / −14 calories = **177 kcal retained**

versus

1 slice cheesecake

257 kcal — 0 g fiber x 4 cal/g / −0 calories — −7 calories per gram of fiber / −0 calories = **257 kcal retained**

Low-Carb Diets

The Paleo diet is one example of a low-carb diet people follow to lose weight. But are you really going to never eat any beans, potatoes, grains, or grain products (like bread)? Every culture on Earth eats grains. I think a better name for this diet would be The Mars diet.

Other examples of low-carb diets are the Zone, the South Beach Diet, Eat Right for Your Type (blood type), and Atkins. They differ in how many carbs they allow, as well as in what carbohydrate foods are considered "good," but they are all different versions of the same concept: that by eating fewer carbs, you'll lose weight.

One of the tricks to a low-carb diet is that when your body believes it's starving, it enters a "starvation state." This happens because our bodies ar designed to run on carbohydrates, and when we deprive them of their prime fuel, they assume we're on a prolonged fast, or even enduring a famine. In order to stay alive, the body starts breaking down its own muscle and fat tissue. When the fat is broken down to create ketones (an emergency substitute for blood sugar, or glucose), we lose body fat and, therefore, lots of weight. Yet we are also losing muscle tissue, which lowers our metabolism in the long run. Worse yet, ketone acids cause bone loss and kidney stones, and can even cause heart disease and birth defects in women who are in early pregnancy.

Running on Carbs

Our bodies are made to be fueled primarily by carbohydrates, and carbs come mostly from plant-based foods. Our teeth, our mouths, our brains, our hormones, the pH balance of our stomachs, our colons, our arteries, even our cells are all made for a fibrous, carb-based diet.

Let's start with the teeth. Human teeth are designed for chopping and grinding things like grains and vegetables, even potatoes and sweet potatoes. Compare your canine teeth to your dog's or cat's. Can yours tear through raw flesh? Don't try it anyway.

Our mouths contain amalase, an enzyme for breaking down carbohydrates ranging from mother's milk to fruit, vegetables, whole grains, and legumes. This is why you hardly have to chew bread. Thanks to amalase it practically melts in your mouth.

The brain runs on glucose, which comes only from carbohydrates. A steady dose (regulated by fiber) protects against diabetes, and it guarantees brain food throughout the day.

Insulin and glucagon are two important hormones. One delivers glucose into cells, the other releases it from liver and muscle stores.

Plant-based foods promote an alkaline pH, helping to neutralize stomach acid and preventing ulcers.

The colon doesn't do so well without a fibrous diet. Fiber is only found in plant-based foods. Unless you eat egg shells.

The cells and arteries rely on plant based food to stay healthy. Cholesterol and saturated fat that come from animal-origin foods make cell membranes harden and become insulin resistant. On the contrary, monounsaturated and Omega-3 fats found in plant based food do the opposite, making cells insulin-sensitive, thus preventing diabetes. Cholesterol and saturated fat also contribute to arterial plaque, while monounsaturated fat and Omega-3 fats increase artery elasticity, or flexibility.

We should all have diets that are high in carbohydrates, since fruit, veggies, whole grains, nuts, peas, seeds, beans, and lentils are primarily composed of carbs. If we were to eat more of these foods, we would get plenty of protein and the good fats (like Omega-3 and monounsaturated fat). And we'd be consuming just the right ratio of carbs to protein to fat. About 70 percent of our calories would be good carbs, 10 to 15 percent would be protein, and 10 to 15 percent would be fat. We wouldn't need to worry a bit about combining "proteins" with "carbs" at each meal, because it would happen naturally.

So let's stay on planet Earth and eat the "good" carbohydrates, like whole grains, unpeeled potatoes and brown rice.

The Short List

Fiber is getting famous, and it's about time. But with all the positive attention fiber has been getting lately, food manufacturers are starting to add refined fiber to many foods, making things like tortillas, bread, and cereals look good on the label. Fiber should not be added; it should be found naturally in food.

The best bet is to buy foods with a short list of ingredients. The fewer ingredients, the more fresh and whole that food is likely to be. The more ingredients, the more preservatives and artificial flavoring agents, and the fewer nutrients that food will naturally contain.

It is legal for food manufacturers to advertise their products as "whole wheat" even if only 25 percent of the flour is actually whole wheat. So read the label. If the first ingredient listed is "enriched flour," the bread product you're buying is made primarily of white, nutrient-depleted flour. So get the real deal, and make sure your bread has at least 3 grams of fiber per slice.

One more tip on bread and bread products: buy fresh. Once grains have been ground into flour, the nutrients are more easily oxidized and therefore lost. The fresher the bread, the more nutrients it will retain. So look for bread products that are made locally and recently.

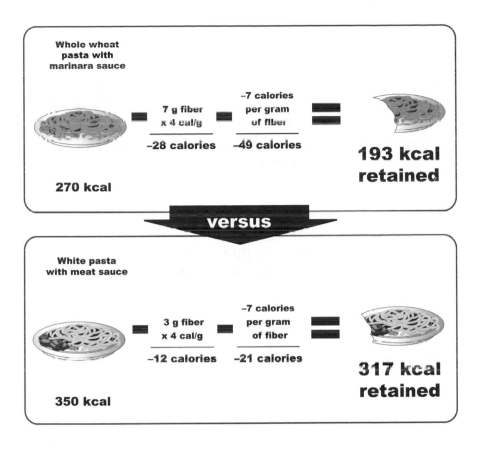

If your local supermarket doesn't carry truly whole-wheat bread, ask the manager to get it. Or purchase your bread from a local bakery or bread store. Or shop at a health-food store. You could also purchase a bread machine and make your own fresh, healthy bread. It's taken me years to discover how easy it is to make my own bread. With a bread machine all I do is add the ingredients and, voila: fresh bread and my house smells like a bakery. (Not to mention, homemade bread really impresses people.)

You're Worth It

These alternatives will likely cost more time or money. But a thinner, disease-free body that doesn't end up in a rest home, on dialysis, or in chemotherapy is priceless. Spend what it takes now and save later. And if you're a typical American, you can probably cut back a little on your entertainment or wardrobe budget to make up the difference.

I have made healthy food a priority in my life. I spend less money on clothes and entertainment. I shop at thrift stores for clothes (and get some amazing deals), and get all my books from the library. And my family spends very little money on movies, eating out, or cable television.

Americans spend less money per capita on food than any other country in the world. And less money is spent on food in this country now than at any time in history. We are simply accustomed to cheap food. Yet good food isn't cheap, nor should it be. The reason we are used to low prices for food is because the livestock and agriculture industries are heavily subsidized by the government. Food in Europe and other western countries costs significantly more because it is less subsidized (or not at all). So don't be deceived. Be willing to invest in your health. Besides, sleep and water are practically free.

Eggs

You may have heard that studies show it's fine to eat an egg a day. These "studies" are sponsored in part by organizations with a vested interest in the outcome. Such studies are set up with an inherent bias, making it easy for the cholesterol from eggs to seem harmless, but regular consumption of eggs is anything but.

One impartial study found men who ate one or more eggs a day were at higher risk for overall mortality. Egg consumption was particularly dangerous for diabetics: those who ate the most eggs were twice as likely to die as those who consumed the least.[1]

Eggs are very high in cholesterol. They are on par with organ meats like liver. Eggs are unfertilized chicken ovum, so they're actually made of steroid hormones (derived from cholesterol) designed to produce and grow a baby chick. Eggs are also loaded with animal protein, which is the last thing the typical Western diet needs.

In addition to cholesterol, toxins such as pesticides, polycholonated biphenals (PCBs), mercury, dioxin, chloride, perchlorate, and others concentrate at higher levels as we go up the food chain. Eggs are way up on the food chain.

Eggs are also contaminated with salmonella. Getting sick from food poisoning is not a key to eating healthy and free. And eggs do not have much in the way of nutrients compared to plant foods. So why eat them?

Lots of recipes call for eggs, but turn out great even if you don't add them. There are some easy replacements, including applesauce, peanut butter, mashed banana, and store-bought egg substitutes. The main purpose for adding eggs in baking is to bind dry ingredients. By adding a little more oil or water to the recipe, dry ingredients will often bind together perfectly.

Cholesterol

Cholesterol is only found in animal-origin foods. Plants cannot produce cholesterol, but all animals do, even in their milk and eggs.

I find it amusing when I see a label on peanut butter that says the product contains no cholesterol. Really? Unless someone's added lard to the peanut butter, there can't be cholesterol, since peanuts are plants.

Let's sort out the facts between "good" versus "bad" cholesterol:

There is no "good" cholesterol found in food. High levels of cholesterol in our diet are always bad.

It is unnecessary to consume cholesterol from food.

Saturated fats are found in all foods (although at lower levels in plant foods), and they convert in our bodies to the cholesterol we need in order to live.

Good cholesterol is transported through the bloodstream inside High Density Lipoprotein (HDL), which eventually leaves the body. Bad cholesterol is carried by Low-Density Lipoproteins (LDL) that deposit cholesterol in our cell membranes or artery linings.

More important than our total cholesterol level is our ratio of LDLs to HDLs. A ratio of four LDLs to one HDL is good, but the smaller the ratio the better (3:1, 2:1). Good cholesterol should be at least 60 mg/dl or more. Low levels of HDL (below 40 mg/dl) are strong predictors of heart disease.

Butter versus Margarine

Butter is full of saturated fat and cholesterol, both of which can raise LDL (bad cholesterol) in the body. But margarine is comprised of partially hydrogenated oils or trans fats, which also convert to LDL cholesterol. So what to do?

Luckily, living in the 21st century means we have options. The best is to use spreads that resemble margarine but are made in ways that don't produce trans fats (usually the oil is expeller-pressed). These are the margarine-looking containers that say, "0 grams trans fat" or, "No partially hydrogenated oils." My favorite brand is Earth Balance. It tastes just like butter. Almost everyone I invite to dinner asks me the name of my "margarine" because they find it so scrumptious!

Here's a short list (more in the appendix) of whole grains and their fiber count:

1 cup brown rice: 4 grams

1 cup whole wheat pasta noodles: 6 grams

5 cups popcorn: 6 grams

1 slice whole grain bread: 3–5 grams

1 cup whole grain cereal: 5–10 grams

THE LOWDOWN ON BEVERAGES

You've probably heard that drinking at least eight glasses (two liters, or sixty-four ounces) of water a day is beneficial, but did you know that water intake is also associated with weight loss? Not only will consuming lots of water help move all that fiber out the back door, it will increase your metabolism, help regulate your appetite, and knock off loads of calories. It will also boost your energy level and combat joint pain. Drinking enough water has even been shown to help prevent cancers of all sorts, including bladder, colon and breast cancer.[1]

Keeping well hydrated is a key to being naturally thin. And unfortunately, it's all too uncommon.

Dehydration — even when we don't feel thirsty — is the number-one cause of headaches and daytime fatigue. Sound familiar?

When we don't consume enough water each day, we retain more calories than we should. Studies show that when we are even slightly dehydrated, our brains begin to confuse thirst with hunger, resulting in an artificially inflated appetite. Have you ever found yourself hungry but once you had something to drink, you realized you were only thirsty? It happens to most Americans every day, but few realize they are thirsty, so they overeat instead.

Another side effect of not consuming enough water is that our fat metabolism slows down. When the kidneys don't have enough water to do their job, they hijack the liver to help them out. When the liver is overworked, it cannot perform its other jobs as effectively. Aside from keeping us alive, I think you'll agree that one of the liver's most important jobs is burning fat efficiently.

Calories from beverages don't make us full; they make us fat. Studies show that when we eat, the chewing motion sends a message to our brains that we're becoming full. Drinking doesn't involve chewing, so no message of satiety is sent to the brain.

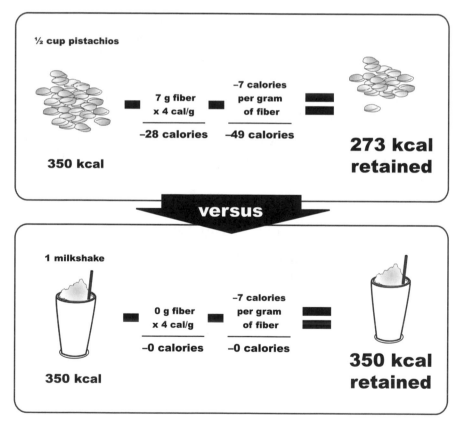

One study at Purdue University put participants on a "jellybean diet." These lucky folks got to eat 450 calories of jellybeans every day for a month. They kept a record of all the other foods they ate, both before and during the study period. At the end of the month, none of the participants had gained any weight. They compensated for all the extra calories by eating less other foods so they consumed the same number of calories as before the study began.

After that first month, the researchers switched those 450 calories from jellybeans to soda, or "liquid jellybeans". Now the participants packed on the weight. Because drinking didn't fulfill their appetites as much as eating, they ate the same number of calories as before they study began, but took in an additional 450 calories a day from drinking soda.[2]

In the US, soft drinks are the fifth largest source of calories for adults.

You already know soda doesn't help you lose weight. So maybe you drink juice, sweetened iced tea, café mocha, lattes, or energy and sports drinks. However healthy your beverage may seem (unless it's mineral water), those calories aren't doing their job to make you full. If you have a craving for sweets, please, eat those sweets, don't drink them.

If you've been consuming a lot of liquid calories and you switch to getting your calories only or mostly from food, be prepared to lose some serious weight.

Let's say you currently consume one eight-ounce glass of juice and one sixteen-ounce café mocha a day. That's a little over four hundred calories. If you forgo the juice and change the mocha into a single-shot espresso, you won't be consuming any calories from drinks. You just cut out four hundred calories a day. One pound of body fat is comprised of 3,500 calories. So in less than nine days, you will lose one pound. Nine days after that, you'll lose another. In a year, you will have lost just over forty pounds – just from taking out two little beverages.

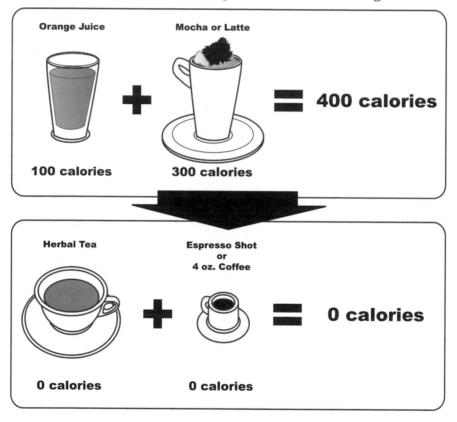

3,500 calories = 1 lb. fat
3,500 calories ÷ 400 calories = 9 days

1 lb. fat loss every 9 days =
40 lb. fat loss in 1 year

Sound too good to be true? Let's do it again.

Let's say you drink one 150-calorie soda in the afternoon and two glasses of wine every evening, but you're only willing to give up one of them. Fine. That five-ounce glass of wine contains 125 calories. So if you cut out the soda and one glass of wine, you're removing 275 calories. That means you'll lose your first pound in just under thirteen days, and more than twenty-eight pounds in a year, just by making this tiny change.

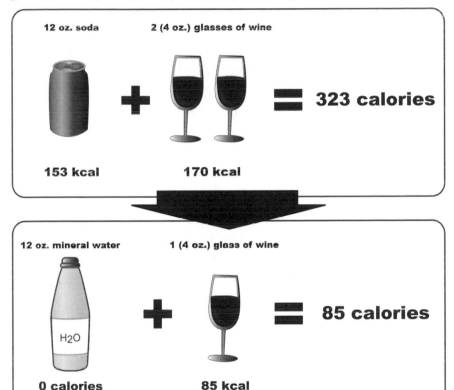

12 oz. soda	2 (4 oz.) glasses of wine	
153 kcal	170 kcal	**323 calories**

12 oz. mineral water	1 (4 oz.) glass of wine	
0 calories	85 kcal	**85 calories**

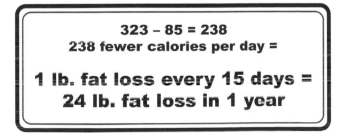

323 – 85 = 238
238 fewer calories per day =

**1 lb. fat loss every 15 days =
24 lb. fat loss in 1 year**

By drinking water in place of beverages that have calories, you are setting yourself up for permanent, powerful weight loss.

When I was teaching on this subject in a college nutrition class, a skinny young student shared his experience with the class. "A couple of years ago, I was drinking four to five sodas a day. Needless to say, I was overweight. I decided to stop drinking soda altogether and switch to water. The first month, I lost twenty-five pounds. The second month, I lost another twenty pounds. I stuck with it for a year or so. Then I began to drink lemonade instead of water. I gained all the weight back in no time. So I switched back to water, and in a few months I dropped forty-five pounds."

I can't begin to tell you how many similar stories I have heard.

Diet Drinks

I was recently asked if there's anything wrong with soda if it's caffeine and sugar free. Trust me, caffeine and sugar are the least dangerous of the chemicals in diet soda. Diet sodas contain either aspartame (found in NutraSweet) or Splenda. Both are toxic.

These artificial sweeteners make your brain think your body is consuming real sugar. Lots of it, because ounce for ounce, these sweeteners are between 200 and 700 times sweeter than sugar.[3] Our bodies prepare for loads of sugar coming into the blood by producing insulin. So now you've got all this insulin sitting in your bloodstream, ready to go to work, but there's no sugar for it to work on. This creates an urgent message to the brain that creates a craving for sugar and refined carbohydrates.

Have you ever noticed that when you drink a diet beverage you crave sweets? There's a chemical connection.

The American Cancer Society has documented that people who use artificial sweeteners gain more weight than people who do not because their appetites are being artificially inflated.[4]

One woman approached me after my seminar to thank me for making sense of her weight loss. She and her friend found diet sodas addictive, so they formed a pact to quit together. After the first week, both women lost five pounds, but had no idea why. Now they knew: their appetites had returned to "normal" without the artificial sweeteners.

Diet sodas can contribute to insulin resistance, which leads to type II diabetes. One way to make insulin ineffective is by triggering it at the wrong times over and over again.

Artificial sweeteners also overstimulate brain cells. That's why you taste more sweetness. Over time, overstimulation can cause those cells to die. The same thing happens to nerve cells. The active ingredient in diet sodas is aspertate, an amino acid that naturally occurs in food and in our bodies. It doesn't actually add flavor, but it is so concentrated in diet sodas that it stimulates the nerve cells to perceive more sweet flavor. Aspartame has been linked with many nervous-system disorders such as Alzheimer's, Parkinson's, Lou Gehrig's disease, multiple sclerosis, and dementia, not to mention migraines.[5]

Most dark sodas also contain phosphoric acid, which is a major cause of bone loss. So you could conclude that all soda is evil and should be poured into a deep pit filled with soda-drinking vipers.

MSG

MSG, or Mono-Sodium Glutamate, works just like aspertate. The concentration of glutamate over-stimulates brain cells so we perceive more flavor in foods. In the process, it can destroy nervous tissue. MSG is used by the food industry as a cheap flavoring agent, and without it, most processed foods would have very little taste.

I once sat next to a lawyer for the food industry on an airplane. As I tried to dig secret industry information out of him, he confessed MSG likely plays a role in childhood obesity. Because foods with MSG contain so much more flavor than real foods, like fruit and vegetables, he believed – as do many health professionals – foods with MSG can be addictive.

Currently, food manufacturers do not have to print MSG on the label. Because MSG is found in many food additives, it is nearly impossible to know which foods contain it. The following is a list of additives containing MSG. But the best way to avoid this chemical is to cut out processed foods as much as possible.

- o   Glutamate
- o   Glutamic acid
- o   Monosodium Glutamate
- o   Textured Protein
- o   Hydrolyzed Protein
- o   Monopotassium Glutamate
- o   Calcium Caseinate
- o   Sodium Caseinate
- o   Gelatin
- o   Yeast Extract
- o   Yeast Food
- o   Autolyzed Yeast

Energy Drinks

Sports drinks are a rip-off. So they're fortified with vitamins and electrolytes (minerals such as potassium and sodium). But the same is true of a piece of fruit and a glass of water, which is cheaper and more beneficial. Sports drinks also contain a lot of calories. In addition, most have artificial colors and flavors that act as excitotoxins.

The name "energy drink" implies that drinking it will give you more energy. But energy literally means "calories." And most energy drinks have caffeine. So come to think of it, these drinks aren't very different from soda. Energy drinks have added vitamins and herbal extracts that presumably raise energy levels. But nutrients from your diet (B vitamins and phytochemicals from whole-plant foods) are more likely to give you more energy, especially if you are currently deficient in these nutrients.

What about smoothies and vegetable drinks? Many commercially produced smoothies contain artificial sweeteners (such as Splenda) that mess with your insulin and therefore your appetite. And since drinking calories, no matter how nutritious, doesn't make us feel as full as eating them, these beverages are not helpful when it comes to losing weight.

So, what should you drink for an afternoon pick-me-up? Try taking a British "tea-time". You could invite your coworkers. Tea time is officially 4pm, but I'm sure there's wiggle-room.

I drink green tea, but black tea has lots of benefits too. There are some delicious tea options out there. Just one caveat: If you want to get away from drinking your calories, drink either unsweetened or lightly sweetened tea (sweetened with raw sugar or honey).

If you go out for tea, be on guard. Many of today's popular coffee vendors offer tea with a lot of needless calories added via milk, cream, and sugar. For example, a chai latte contains black tea and spices, but it also has a lot of milk and sugar (averaging 200 to 300 calories). Lightly sweetened black tea gives great pick-me-up with very few calories.

Tasty Water

If you want to replace flavored beverages with water, get yourself some tasty water.

For example, if you're currently drinking hot mochas or lattes, don't even think about just switching to plain water – look for the best-tasting tea or coffee you can find. These days there are a lot of good choices. If you find some that taste good without adding cream or much sugar, it will be far more likely to stick.

For me, a few tablespoons of vanilla-flavored soymilk taste great in a cup of fresh-brewed coffee. I've also found some herbal teas that taste good without adding anything. (Peppermint is my favorite.)

If you want to cut back on soda, find a naturally flavored (lime, lemon, orange) mineral water. If you're trying to cut out a cold sugary drink, replace it with unsweetened iced tea. If it's juice, add slices of lemon or orange to filtered water or iced tea. Or try a flavored iced tea, like raspberry.

If you try to substitute something you like with something you don't, it won't last. So do a little taste-bud research and find tasty substitutes.

Caffeine

America's favorite drug is caffeine. And I'll admit, when it comes to coffee I'm as American as apple pie.

Coffee by itself has no calories – which is good news. But many of the coffee drinks in this country contain very little coffee but lots of milk and sugar. That makes coffee drinks go from zero to well over two hundred calories. So if you love coffee, drink it black or with a little soy milk.

Coffee is a strong diuretic: you pee out more water than you take in. Black and green teas are less strong since they contain less caffeine. So if you drink a lot of coffee or espresso, even though they have zero calories, you still won't lose weight if you're dehydrated.

Do you have to cut out coffee altogether? Heavens, no. Just make sure you drink no more than one or two eight-ounce servings a day. And you'll need to drink more water to compensate for the liquid you're losing.

I drink coffee every morning. In fact, you might say I have a "habit" of starting my day with coffee (just ask my husband). But I am very cautious about what goes in my coffee. Cow's milk and cream never enter my cup. Nor do I buy fancy coffee drinks containing vast amounts of chocolate or flavor shots. I know my body doesn't register those calories; they don't make me feel full. Neither do they satisfy my sweet tooth like eating real chocolate (which does make me feel full). I just add a little soymilk to my coffee, and if I crave sweets, I eat something sweet along with it. If I'm feeling a little wild, I might even dip that sweet thing into my coffee. Biscotti, anyone?

Alcohol

Alcohol is another beloved diuretic. But alas, wine, beer, and hard liquor can dehydrate your body quickly. Alcohol has other disadvantages in regard to weight loss. It's loaded with calories—seven per gram to be exact. And since you're drinking those calories, you can bet they don't make you full.

Excess calories from alcohol tend to store in the abdomen. That's is where we derive our colloquial "beer belly" (although it might be also called a "wine-" or "tequilla belly"). This is the most dangerous place to store fat. Abdominal fat has been strongly correlated with diabetes, heart disease, and breast cancer.[6] Smokers tend to store more calories in this area as well, greatly increasing their risk of chronic disease.

Alcoholic beverages also tend to overstimulate our appetites, making us feel hungrier than we really are.

So if you love drinking wine at dinner, know you could lose a lot of weight by loving it a little less. One fewer glass a day will go a long way. And don't forget to drink more water to rehydrate.

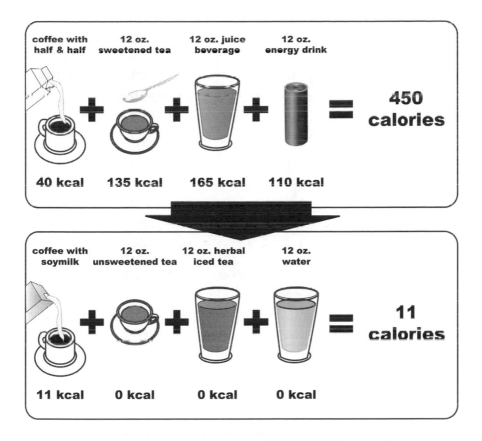

450 – 11 = 439
439 fewer calories per day =

**1 lb. fat loss every 8 days =
45.6 lb. fat loss in 1 year**

Red, Red Wine

Wine, when imbibed in moderation, is known to help prevent heart disease. Like all alcohol, wine is a vasodilator; therefore, it improves blood flow for a limited amount of time. This increases the body's circulation of blood and oxygen to the cells. Red wine has also been noted for the antioxidant properties of its flavonoids.[7]

But wine (like all alcohol) is a diuretic, so you lose water and electrolytes every time you drink it. Those electrolytes are essential for controlling blood pressure and preventing bone loss. If you consume alcohol excessively, you will eventually suffer from high blood pressure and premature bone loss.

All that pressure on your arteries creates tears to the arterial tissue, which results in plaque. Arterial plaque slows down blood flow, causing the heart to pump harder to compensate, resulting in even higher blood pressure.

Because alcohol in excess is toxic, it creates free radicals in the body as the liver works to detoxify it. Those free radicals can cause cancer. They also injure the arterial lining, leading to more plaque.

So although wine does contain beneficial antioxidants, let's be moderate in our wine consumption. And if it's really just the health benefits you're after, you can always eat grapes.

9 LEARN FROM THE SUMO WRESTLERS

Have you ever thought how astute sumo wrestlers are in maintaining their weight? Bigger is better in the sumo world and since wrestlers average 450 pounds, you know they're doing something right. If we could learn their secrets, then do the opposite, we could lose some serious weight.

You may think sumo wrestlers eat all day long. But the opposite is true. They eat only one meal a day. That's right: one big-ass meal.

When we eat only once or twice a day, the body thinks it's starving, so it lowers its metabolism. When those calories do come in, they are more likely to be retained as fat than calories that come in more frequently. In addition, the body produces appetite-enhancing hormones that remind us to eat – and eat. So if we eat only one or two meals a day, we will more than compensate for the meals we skipped. In fact, ninety percent of obese Americans eat two or fewer meals a day.

If you know anyone who eats fewer than three meals a day, you might want to tell them they're on the Sumo Wrestler Diet. I'll bet they'll really appreciate it.

Breakfast

Breakfast is famous for being the "most important meal of the day". That's because eating breakfast jump-starts your metabolism, keeping it going at a faster rate all day long. How cool is that? You eat more and you lose weight.

The word breakfast indicates that we are breaking a fast. While we sleep (assuming we're not sleep-snacking in the middle of the night), we're fasting. While our metabolism doesn't turn off completely when we sleep, it does slow down. After eight to ten hours of fasting, if we skip breakfast, our metabolism will remain in starvation mode, which means a slower metabolism throughout the day.

A friend of mine started eating breakfast after I told her about this. She didn't make any other changes in her diet. She lost seven pounds the first month.

Breakfast doesn't have to be eaten before you leave the house in the morning. There is no official "cut off" time for breakfast, except before lunch (or maybe 10:30am). You can bring a peanut butter sandwich or smoothie to work and eat it anytime during the morning. Doesn't that sound better than scarfing down a bowl of cereal in the wee morning hours?

When you do eat breakfast, you may feel famished before lunchtime. But that's a good thing. It means your metabolism is running faster. When your body tells you to eat more, obey. Since your metabolism goes up every time you eat (called thermogenesis), people who eat regular meals and snacks throughout the day will actually burn more calories. And frequently ingested calories are less likely to become fat. Remember, if sumo wrestlers eat one meal a day, your strategy needs to be just the opposite.

Are you ready to hear something extremely profound? The world's best appetite suppressant is food. Who would have guessed? When we go hours and hours without eating, we overeat at the next meal, and end up eating something we'd rather avoid. But when we always have a little something in our belly, we don't go crazy at mealtime. That's because our blood sugar isn't too low and we're not producing those appetite-enhancing hormones. Eating regularly keeps us stable, centered, and rational (as possible), and it keeps our metabolism from slowing down. Eating small, frequent meals and snacks throughout the day is key to being naturally thin.

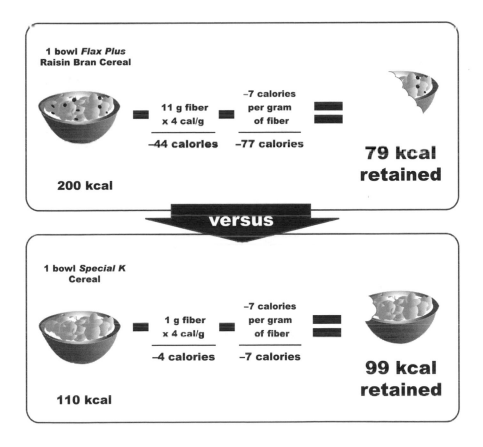

Grazers

Do you know people who don't obsess about food or weight, are always eating, but are trim and healthy? These are the people we love to hate. It seems unfair that they can be slender but eat so often. You might think it's genetic, but that's usually not the case. These folks are bonafide "grazers."

Most naturally thin people graze on food throughout the day. They eat when they're hungry – and get this – *only* when they're hungry. They don't eat because they're bored, restless, lonely, or anxious. They eat when they feel hunger pangs in their stomachs, or if they notice their blood sugar is low (when everything turns black when they stand up quickly, or they become moody after they haven't eaten for a while, especially in the afternoon).

Grazers stop eating when they feel full. But first let's redefine that word: full. In our modern American vernacular, "full" usually means we got our money's worth at an all-you-can-eat buffet. But that's way beyond full – that's "stuffed".

Being "full" doesn't mean feeling bloated or uncomfortable after eating. As a matter of fact, full is not a feeling at all, but rather the absence of a feeling: the absence of hunger. Naturally thin grazers eat when they're hungry and stop when they're no longer hungry. And when they are bored, restless, lonely and anxious, they do something other than eat. Some call a friend or go for a walk. When I feel restless and head toward the kitchen, my saving grace is in making a cup of tea, teapot and all. This gives me something to do with my hands – besides eat – and I still get to be in my favorite room in the house. I find sipping a mug of hot tea very comforting.

The New Definition of "Full"

Grazing requires eating more slowly than most of us are used to so we know when we are no longer hungry. When we eat at record pace, who knows when we became full.

If we listen to our bodies, eating when we're hungry and stopping when we're no longer hungry, we will eat small, frequent meals and snacks. And the self-discipline of stopping is easier than you think. If you find it hard to stop eating, just remind yourself that you'll be hungry again in a few hours, and you can finish your meal then.

There are amazing benefits to being an adult. Many of us grew up with siblings who would take our favorite food or candy from us, so if we liked something, we had to eat it all fast. But as adults, we don't have to continue this "now or never" relationship with food. (In fact, next time you sit down to eat, look around to see if anyone is waiting to steal your food. You might be happily surprised.) So we can slow down and savor our food. We can put leftovers in a box and eat them later. Worst-case scenario: if someone eats our leftovers, we can go buy more. Adults have purchasing power.

Carolyn

My college roommate Carolyn was beautiful and thin. She didn't exercise, and she wasn't obsessed with her weight. On the other hand, I was on the thicker side, even though I exercised like crazy. And I was the nutrition major. It wasn't pretty (well, she was pretty), and I often wondered why God put us in the same apartment.

So I did what any self-respecting young woman would do: I watched Carolyn like a hawk. One night at dinner I realized something. Being raised to eat everything on my plate (you know, to save starving children around the world), I always finished my dinner. Carolyn, on the other hand, stopped eating about halfway through her meal. She said she was full and that she would finish her food later. I was speechless. What about her duty to fight world hunger?

Sure enough, several hours later, Carolyn went back to the kitchen and heated up her leftovers. What was one large meal for me were two small meals for her. That was how Carolyn ate all the time. She snacked, or ate small meals, throughout the day. When she was distressed or bored, she didn't turn to food; she called a friend, practiced music, or played solitaire (she really did).

When the two of us went on a road trip together, we stopped at practically every mini-mart along the way. No joke. Whenever Carolyn felt hungry, she got off the freeway in search of a snack, which was frequently. Even though I found it inconvenient, Carolyn was keeping her metabolism going. Eventually I convinced her to buy a bunch of snacks to stash in the back seat, which made us both happier.

Dried fruit, nuts, seeds, and trail mix make great, high-fiber snacks for road trips (or everyday commutes). Energy bars that are made primarily from dried fruit, nuts, and whole grains, and not overly processed, are also good alternatives. When you have these "fast foods" placed strategically in your car or bag, you'll find it less tempting to pull over for real fast food.

After Hours

What about snacking at night? Most of us figure when we eat late in the evening, we won't be burning off those calories since we'll just be going to sleep. Thus, eating late is taboo. But what if you're really hungry at ten p.m.? Will the calories from what you eat turn into an extra roll around your belly by morning?

Although our metabolism slows down while we sleep, it doesn't turn off completely. If you go to bed hungry, your nighttime metabolism will actually be lower than if you had eaten.

Many people find that if they eat just before bedtime, they wake up ravenous. But that's a good thing. That means their metabolism sped up significantly during the night. And remember, we want to do the opposite of The Sumo Wrestler Diet. Eating more frequently is exactly that. Hunger signals help us along this path – so listen to those pangs. And know the only wrong time to eat is when you're not hungry.

WHY DAIRY IS SCARY

Dairy products are plain confusing. Advertisements claim that dairy products can help us lose weight. We hear about the "good" bacteria in yogurt. We are told how much calcium we need to prevent osteoporosis. Sounds like dairy is a good, even necessary, part of our diet. But is it?

Did you know that those commercials telling us that dairy consumption causes weight loss were pulled from the airwaves? In May 2007, the Federal Trade Commission announced they would be discontinued since such claims are not supported by conclusive evidence.[1]

Mammals concentrate toxins in their milk. So we get extremely high levels of mercury, perchlorate, PCBs, pesticides, and dioxin in milk and dairy products. Organic dairy products aren't much better. While they aren't fed or sprayed with pesticides, they still get toxins through water, air, and runoff from other farms.

A 2007 study from the American Journal of Epidemiology links the consumption of dairy products to an increased risk for Parkinson's disease. Researchers investigated the association between dairy products and risk among 388 men and women diagnosed with Parkinson's disease. Results showed that as dairy product consumption increased, risk for Parkinson's also increased. Those who consumed the most dairy milk had a 70 percent greater risk for the disease.[2]

One study from Germany shows that dairy product consumption may increase the risk of testicular cancer. Researchers at the University of Halle-Wittenberg tracked dietary contributors to testicular cancer among 269 men with cancer and 797 control subjects. The risk for testicular cancer was increased by 37 percent for those who consumed at least twenty servings of milk per month.[3]

And if that weren't scary enough, many studies have linked dairy products with prostate cancer.[4]

Because mammals concentrate toxins in their milk, dairy products are loaded with toxic substances.[5] Toxins have "endocrine-mimicking properties," meaning they imitate steroid, or reproductive, hormones such as estrogen in humans. Ironically, people avoid soymilk because they've heard misinformed hype about plant estrogens, so instead they drink cow's milk, which is loaded with estrogen-mimicking substances. Commercial cow milk not only contains toxins that act like hormones, but it has added hormones and antibiotics. Even organic cow milk has naturally occurring growth hormones.

Taking dairy products out of my diet enabled me to lose fifteen pounds over a year's time, even though my aim was avoiding toxins and cancer (not that I'm complaining now). I wasn't consuming a lot to begin with: milk in my cereal each morning, yogurt and cheese every now and then. I still eat cheese on rare occasions, but mostly soy cheese (Follow Your Heart brand), and I enjoy soy yogurt and soymilk.

As for the beneficial bacteria in yogurt, know the same bacteria are found in soy-based yogurt. So you can have it all: healthy bacteria without toxins and excess estrogen.

IGF-1 Hormone

One well-known growth hormone found in cow's milk is IGF-1 (Insulin-Like Growth Factor). This steroid is found in meats and cow milk as well as human milk. It's great at helping newborn cows and humans grow, but when we get older, it's downright carcinogenic.

Here are a few quotes in scientific journals regarding IGF-1 and cancer:

The insulin-like growth factor-1 (IGF-1) system...has been implicated to play a critical role in the development of breast cancer.[6]

In light of recent epidemiological studies correlating high circulating levels of IGF-1 with increased risk of second primary tumors of the head and neck...[7]

High serum concentrations of insulin-like growth factor-1 (IGF-1) are associated with an increased risk of breast, prostate, colorectal, and lung cancer...[8]

The insulin-like growth factors (IGFs) are potent mitogens for breast cancer cells...[9]

Studies have shown that IGFs are potent mitogens for a variety of cancer cells including prostate cancer since they stimulate cancer cell growth and suppress programmed cell death.[10]

Recent epidemiologic investigations have suggested an association between increased blood levels of insulin-like growth factor 1 (IGF-1) and increased risk of prostate cancer.[11]

Insulin-like growth factors… are thought to be significant factors involved in normal and malignant cellular proliferation including… prostate cancer.[12]

Estrogen and insulin/IGF-1 differentially regulate c-Myc and cyclin D1 to cooperatively stimulate breast cancer cell proliferation.[13]

It was found that the increase of IGF-1 level was followed by a 3.15-fold increased risk for developing colon cancer.[14]

Milk intake also raises serum levels of insulin-like growth factor-I (IGF-I).[15]

Dairy products contain both hormones and growth factors, in addition to fat and various chemical contaminants that have been implicated in the proliferation of human breast cancer cells.[16]

Thanks to vested interests, you've probably never heard of this hormone before. Now that you have, do you really want to consume much in the way of dairy products?

Calcium and Bones

So now you're wondering, "If I take out dairy, how will I get the calcium I need?"

Most milk alternatives, such as rice, almond and soymilk are calcium-fortified with amounts equivalent to milk. Also, contrary to popular belief, dairy products are a poor source of calcium, nor do we need anywhere near the 1,000 to 1,300 milligrams of calcium a day recommended by the Institute of Medicine (IOM) of the National Academy of Sciences.

The IOM recommends we consume that much calcium to compensate for all the calcium we lose eating a typical American diet. If we were to decrease the amount of calcium we lose, we would no longer "need" so much calcium from our diet. So let's look at what causes calcium depletion from our bodies.

The biggest calcium thief is animal protein. Consuming animal protein creates an imbalance of uric and sulfuric acid in our blood, forcing the body to neutralize these acids by releasing calcium from our bones. The calcium buffers the acid, but is then released into our urinary tract, where it either winds up in the toilet or builds up in the kidney — the major reason for kidney stones.

One study followed over 1,000 elderly women for seven years. They placed women in three categories according to their diet: those with a high ratio of animal to vegetable protein, a middle range, and a low range. The study found women consuming the most animal protein had nearly four times the rate of hip fractures when compared to those who consumed the least animal protein.[17]

Another study that tracked over 8,000 women found those who consumed the most animal protein incurred significant bone loss, while women who consumed diets high in plant protein had virtually no bone loss.[18]

A second major calcium reducer is dark soda. Almost all colas — diet, regular, or caffeine free — contain high concentrations of phosphoric acid. This acid has an antagonistic relationship to calcium, and when consumed at concentrated levels, causes calcium to be lost. Other common calcium depleters are excess sodium, alcohol, and caffeine.

Studies done in rural parts of Asia and Africa found that elderly women tend to consume little or no dairy products. Their calcium consumption is only 300-600 milligrams per day. Yet these women have extremely low rates of osteoporosis. Researchers believe this to be due to the low amounts of "calcium losers" in their diet, including animal protein, processed foods, and soda. Genetic relatives of these populations, consuming an American diet, have the same rates of osteoporosis as Americans do, so diet and lifestyle

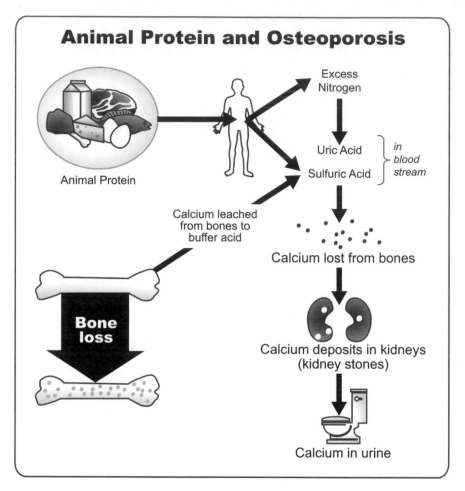

After finding elderly South African Bantu women had stronger bones – in spite of lifelong low calcium intake, numerous pregnancies and long lactation periods – than Caucasian elderly women, one researcher concluded, "it is questioned whether the present insistence on a high calcium intake is justified."[20]

Excess calcium from dairy products (as well as calcium supplements) also competes with other minerals for absorption in the body and lowers the uptake of minerals such as iron, zinc, magnesium, and copper. Many of these minerals play an essential role in building and maintaining bone. A leading cause of iron-deficiency anemia in children is too much milk.[21]

The 12-year Nurses' Health Study followed 78,000 women, finding no association between milk consumption and bone density. In fact, the risk of hip fracture for women who drank two or more glasses of milk a day was 1.45 times more than for those who rarely drank milk.[22]

Reviewing 20 major calcium trials in postmenopausal women over a 20-year-period, one researcher concluded, "trials in which calcium and estrogen have been directly compared have shown that the latter is generally more effective than calcium in that it produces a small, but often significant bone gain...In older women, the importance of calcium intake is overshadowed by the strong association between vitamin D insufficiency and hip fracture".[23]

Do we really need 1,300 milligrams of calcium daily to prevent bone loss? No indeed. When we cut down on the calcium losers and get enough sunlight (for vitamin D), we need very little.

Bovine proteins

The proteins found in cow milk are indigestible, which means when they enter our bloodstream, they are still in protein form. Our bodies react to protein in the blood as if it is an antigen, or foreign invader, and set off auto-immune reactions in response. That's why, after we drink milk, we find phlegm in our throats. Phlegm, or mucus, is comprised of white blood cells responding as though there were an invader in our digestive tract. This response causes many children to cough often, especially during sleep. Milk consumption is strongly linked with ear infections, frequent colds, and congestion. It's even associated with type 1 diabetes in very young children. In adults, cow-milk proteins are frequently linked to rheumatoid arthritis and other auto-immune disorders.

Bovine proteins are also known for causing intestinal bleeding. This is why giving whole cow milk to infants under one year is dangerous; they lose blood in their stools and rapidly become anemic. Intestinal blood loss occurs in older children as well, which is why milk is the number-one cause for childhood anemia.

My five-year-old has never drunk cow's milk. Her bones are strong, she's tall and slender but not too thin, and she's never had an ear infection. I haven't consumed milk in ten years, and my bones are just as solid as they were in my early twenties.

No other mammal drinks milk from an animal other than its own mother. In the wild, once baby animals are weaned, they never drink milk again. So why is it we humans think we need supplemental milk from a cow after our children are weaned? If I didn't know better, I'd say it's the dairy industry.

Soy Products

Many people think that soy products can cause cancer. However, the opposite has been proven true by many studies. The plant estrogens, or isoflavone compounds in soybeans and soy products actually counteract reproductive cancers.

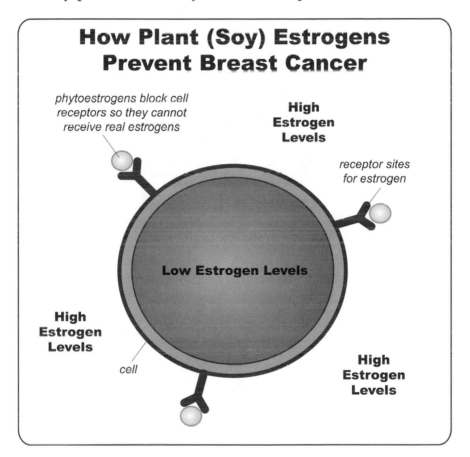

In Japan, researchers conducted a study of 678 women with breast cancer and 3,390 controls matched by age and menopausal status with no history of cancer. They "observed a significantly reduced risk" of breast cancer among the women who ate the most soy and were estrogen receptor, or ER-positive, and HER2 (Human Epidermal Growth Factor Receptor 2)-negative or both. For women who ate the most soy compared with those who ate the least, the odds of having ER-positive breast cancer were reduced by 26 percent, and for women with HER2-negative breast cancer, the reduced risk was 22 percent.

In their own words, the researchers concluded, "These findings are biologically plausible, and suggest a potential benefit of soybean products in the prevention of breast cancer."[24]

Another study published in the American Journal of Epidemiology found that women who consumed three milligrams of isoflavones per day had a 44 percent lower risk of ovarian cancer than those who consumed less than one milligram per day.[25]

Phytoestrogens in soy protect against female reproductive cancers because they act as estrogen antagonists when estrogen levels are dangerously high. The phytoestrogens from soy can block cell receptor cites where estrogen would otherwise enter, thus preventing estrogen levels from climbing too much.

Because a high level of estrogen in the body is linked with breast, endometrial, and ovarian cancer, we need plant estrogens to help regulate this hormone. When our estrogen levels are dangerously low, plant estrogens take on estrogen-mimicking properties, reducing our risk of heart disease and osteoporosis.

As for the impact of plant estrogens on men, there are myriad studies documenting the protective effect of soy products against prostate cancer.[26]

So please don't be afraid of unprocessed soy products like soybeans (edaname), tempeh, tofu, or soymilk. They won't increase your risk of breast cancer or make the men in your life less masculine. Plant estrogens work differently than endogenous (internally-produced) estrogen. Which is a relief, since phytoestrogens are found in fruit, vegetables, and whole grains in addition to soybeans and other legumes.

# BELLY FAT AND BLOOD PRESSURE

Visceral fat is fat around the mid-section - the proverbial spare tire. This is the most dangerous place to carry fat since these fat cells require more blood flow than fat elsewhere. Abdominal fat also makes us more likely to develop hypertension, diabetes, heart disease, and stroke.

Those of us living under chronic stress produce too much of a hormone called cortisol, which heaps on the visceral fat stores. Excessive cortisol can be produced by stressing out our bodies, and not just in the obvious ways. Smoking, excessive caffeine and alcohol consumption, not getting enough sleep, and - would you believe – skipping meals can stress our bodies into making excess cortisol.

Too much cortisol makes us crave sugary and high-fat foods. It causes us to have an unnaturally elevated appetite. And all those extra calories go straight to our gut, putting us at risk of chronic diseases. Excess cortisol can also cause "lipogenesis," the creation of new fat cells, and suppress the immune system.

So let's address stress head on:

Sit-ups don't remove abdominal fat or deal with the root issue of cortisol, so don't even think about them.

- **Deal with the root issues**: get enough sleep, don't drink more than two cups of coffee a day, don't smoke or skip meals, don't overdo alcohol, and get rid of the sources of stress in your life. It's a life-or-death issue.

- **Exercise.** It's good for your heart, and it's an amazing stress release. So start moving. It will change your mind-set and your hormones, even if you don't lose a pound.

- **Being out in nature** relieves stress, so get on out there.

- **Have a great network of friends**. If you don't have friends you can confide in and laugh with, make some. And spend as much time with them as possible.

- **Find a hobby** you can lose yourself in. Music, cooking, sewing or quilting, drawing, painting, writing ... whatever it is, do it whenever you can.

- **Turn off your TV.** Too much television, even when found enjoyable, stresses out the brain and body. Our minds and bodies were made to be active, not passive. Besides, the content of most television shows can contribute to stress, and the commercials entice us to eat more.

- **Read great books.**

- **Help others in need.**

- **Pray.**

All of these things reduce stress and improve the quality of our lives and the lives of others.

Healthy Relaxation

Relaxation is in. Relaxation doesn't just prevent unhealthy levels of cortisol, it helps with digestion – especially in the out-going department, if you know what I mean.

Most people have a bowel movement first thing in the morning, when they're most relaxed. They may have another after they've begun to rest, like when they get home from work, sit down to read a book, or lie down just before bed.

There's a relationship between resting and eliminating. When our body is most relaxed, it's able to eliminate properly.

And you've probably noticed it's hard to "stay regular" when we travel. Traveling can be fun, but our bodies are not relaxed when they're in a new environment.

When our bodies are at rest, other good things happen too. Our immune system is boosted. Our bodies produce good hormones. If you get in an accident, you're less likely to be injured if you're relaxed (or asleep). If your body is relaxed when you fall, you won't get hurt. Pregnant women are most likely to go into labor in the middle of the night, when they are most relaxed.

Our bodies were made to be relaxed, to breathe deeply, and to be at peace. So I command you: relax already.

High Blood Pressure

You already knew stress can cause high blood pressure. But did you know it kills brain cells?

Prolonged high blood pressure kills cells and tissues in your body. Studies show that people who have had long-term hypertension had poorer brain function than those without. Over the long run, high blood pressure leads to Alzheimer's and dementia because it cuts off oxygen to the brain.[1]

Lack of oxygen makes us age prematurely. When oxygen isn't delivered regularly to the cells, it causes impotence, joint inflammation, macular degeneration, and cataracts, not to mention loss of mental acuity. Eventually it will lead to heart attack and stroke.

When most people think of fighting high blood pressure through diet, they think of cutting back on salt. But that's not entirely sound nutrition. Salt is an "extracellular" electrolyte. It resides outside the cells; therefore, it retains water between cells but not inside. This is an important function, and we would die without it.

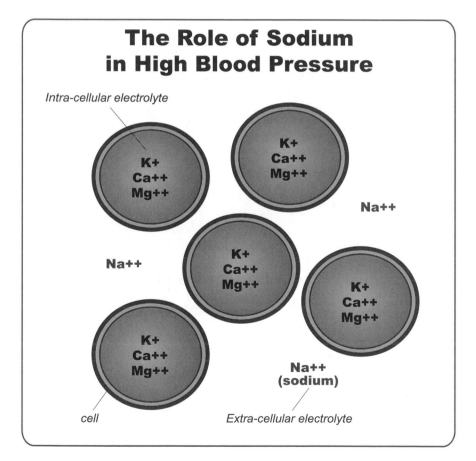

The problem is, most of us get loads of sodium but not enough "intracellular" electrolytes. These minerals retain water inside cells, which prevents an excess of water outside cells, leading to high blood pressure. Three of the best-known intracellular electrolytes are potassium, calcium, and magnesium. Studies show that people with enough potassium, magnesium, and calcium from their diets do not develop high blood pressure even when sodium intake is very high.[2] Which is why I never eat unsalted nuts.

What foods have all these intracellular electrolytes? The same foods that are high in fiber and essential for weight loss: fruits, vegetables, whole grains, and legumes. One study found that vegans (vegetarians who don't consume eggs or dairy products) have only one half to one third the incidence of high blood pressure verses meat-eaters.[3] You don't have to go full-fledged meatless; just eat way less meat and more of the good stuff. Or sure, go meatless. You have my endorsement.

Plaque

Plaque is our body's emergency "patch kit" to an injury or perforation in our arteries. But when our arteries are injured too often, plaque becomes more or less permanent. This causes high blood pressure.

What causes such nasty injuries? Homocysteine and free radicals. High levels of homocysteine are derived from animal protein, and free radicals are produced when we are exposed to or consume toxic chemicals, such as pesticides and mercury. Common products that contain toxic chemicals are household cleaning products, including laundry detergent and fabric softener, perfume and perfumed products such as air fresheners and unnaturally scented candles, soaps and lotions. (One of the reasons certain problems are labeled "hypoallergenic" is because they don't contain perfumes.) By using natural or old-fashioned cleaning products such as baking soda and vinegar we can kill germs without creating free radicals.

The good news is how we eat can also lower these compounds. Folic acid lowers homocysteine levels while antioxidants fight free radicals. Folic acid and antioxidants are found exclusively in fruits, vegetables, whole grains, and legumes. Foods that are fresh, in season, locally grown, vine- or tree-ripened, and organic tend to be more abundant in nutrients and antioxidants than those that are commercially grown.

MAKING IT STICK

Eating healthy takes time and energy, and Lord knows, most of us are short on both. So here are some tips for the day-to-day journey.

Did you know almost half our meals are consumed at restaurants? Americans currently eat out twice as much as 50 years ago – and it shows. The fact that we're too rushed to cook our own food makes airplanes need to widen the girth of their seats, not to mention increasing the cost of airfare. After all, we are not just what, but where we eat.

Who in the world convinced us that we could have it all? And why did we believe it? We can't take a shortcut like not cooking and expect it not to catch up on us. Especially when we're talking about our health. Health takes time. So let's all just slow down and focus on what's important. Health is important because without it, life stinks.

Just so you know where I'm coming from, I'll be honest. I am a total princess and would love to have maids and butlers wait on me all day long. Sometimes I feel like so much of my time is devoted to purchasing, cooking and consuming food that I despair starting another grocery list. I'm no more naturally disciplined than the next gal. But once I push past the princess-ness, it feels good. I actually like figuring out what recipes I'm going to try, making my list and shopping (I love running into people at the store). Most shockingly, I find cooking to be aesthetically pleasing, calming and dare I say, artistic? I also love to share what I've made with friends and acquaintances, allowing me to get to know them better.

Harriet Van Horne wrote, "Cooking is like Love. It should be entered into with abandon or not at all." Sometimes with our busy lives, it can be easy to view cooking as a means to an end... we cook just so that we can eat. But I truly believe that enjoying the process of cooking is just as important as the food itself. Remember: this process is about building healthy habits for the long haul. No matter how good it is for you, if you have a bad attitude, chances are slim you will want to continue. I enjoy cooking most when I put on music and take time to be thankful for all the delicious food I am able to prepare. I also see cooking as time to relax my mind entirely: to focus only on preparing food and forget everything else. Instead of feeling rushed to finish, I claim the kitchen for myself and make it "my time".

Don't let this crazy fast-paced culture we live in rob you of one of the most basic pleasures in life: real food. And your decision will pay you back. I promise.

Cooking Tips for Princes and Princesses

I make my own "convenience" foods by doubling (or tripling) the recipe of every meal I cook. Cooking a greater volume of food takes no more time, but saves hours of work later on. When I'm hungry and don't have time to cook, I have my own "fast food": leftovers in the fridge or freezer. Speaking of leftovers, plan ahead about how to use them efficiently.

No, putting them in a huge Tupperware container with a plate on top because you can't find the lid is not a plan. Instead, try taking the time to separate out individual servings and freeze them for lunches or future dinners. For example, let's say you just cooked a big pot of vegetable chili to eat with cornbread. After dinner, pack up two separate containers of chili, one to freeze and one for the fridge. The next night you might heat the refrigerated chili to put on a baked potato. Over the weekend, pull out the frozen chili and use for nachos with tortilla chips, and avocados. You'd be surprised how easy it is to make multiple meals at one time. And the pay-off is awesome: delicious, homemade meals to bring to work or come home to.

If I don't have time to cook regularly, I designate one or two days (or evenings) in a week just for cooking. For example, Saturdays and Wednesday nights are a great day to spend a few hours in the kitchen, cooking in sweatpants, listening to music. Yes, I know, this might require you to give up some of your free time – but the flip side is your body "gives up" loads of extra pounds. I'd say it's a no-brainer, besides, cooking helps ground us. That's right, cooking is good for our mental health, and who couldn't benefit from that?

These days we spend a great deal of time on the road, which can make healthy eating seem impossible. But did you know there are some very cool food containers that allow us to bring healthy meals with us? I recently stumbled along a two-tier stainless steel container that even has a separate compartment for salad dressing (called To-Go Ware, found at www.to-goware.com). How easy is it to make some salad with garbanzo or kidney beans, dried cranberries, raisins, walnut pieces, sunflower seeds, apple pieces, etc., and carry it with you in your car? Really easy, considering it'd stay fresh and cool in stainless steel – or that you could add the dressing right before you eat. Also, there's plenty of thermos-ware for hot foods that allow us to bring soup, stews and other homemade dishes along with us. So there goes that excuse about being "too busy" to eat right.

My favorite time saving device in the kitchen is a pressure cooker. I use mine mainly to cook beans: garbanzo, pinto, black, white, and kidney. After soaking, beans only take an average of twenty minutes to cook in a pressure cooker, versus an hour and a half on the stove. I recommend soaking beans in water the night before, then draining the water and rinsing the beans prior to cooking to get rid of gas and expedite cooking. (Kombu, a sea vegetable, also helps decrease gas when cooked with beans). Another pitch for pressure cookers: potatoes only take ten to fifteen minutes in a pressure cooker, and artichokes only five minutes. And don't worry, today's pressure cookers have built-in safety devices, unlike grandma's.

My other favorite time saving device is my rice cooker. Like a crockpot, you can put in rice and water, then leave, returning home to freshly steamed hot (brown) rice. It never burns the rice since it will stop cooking when all the water has boiled off.

Another crucial time-saver is a good kitchen knife. Start with a good Chef's Knife since it will do the majority of the cutting and should fit comfortably in your hand. High-carbon stainless steel is best and the size depends on what feels best in your hand. When shopping, actually go through cutting motions with the knife to assess comfort. Be prepared to pay $75 or more for a good knife – it is worth it in the long run.

Another option is to have your kitchen knives sharpened.

Other essential kitchen tools include a good cutting board (best with a grip on the bottom so they don't move around), a stainless steel soup pot, a non-teflon wok, and a good set of measuring cups and spoons.

Well-planned snack foods also save time and needless pounds. Bring high-fiber snacks with you everywhere you go, so you can eat when you're hungry and keep up your metabolism. Great snacks for stashing in your car, desk, locker, and purse include dried fruit, roasted nuts and seeds, and trail mix. That way, instead of being hungry while you drive home and then overeating when you arrive, you'll find your appetite abated and your mood improved. At home, you will be able to enjoy a much smaller dinner, and you'll probably be nicer to the people you live with.

So get in the habit of bringing snacks and water with you everywhere you go. If you've ever cared for a small child, you probably already developed this habit – for the child. Now let's do it for you.

Free to Eat Pantry

There is nothing like a well-stocked pantry. Kitchens should proudly display the beauty of food. Find some glass jars and fill them with bulk dried foods like red and green lentils, beans (garbanzo, white, black, and pinto), split peas, millet, quinoa, barley, brown rice, dried fruit, various nuts and seeds. Buy smaller jars for colorful spices like cinnamon, cardamom, paprika, cumin, cayenne, turmeric, coriander, dill, oregano, thyme, and basil. The next time you are wondering what to cook, you will have beautiful visual reminders surrounding you, saying, "Here I am. Cook me!"

Other pantry staples should include vegetable broth, tahini paste, Thai chili paste (red), coconut milk, cans of whole and crushed tomatoes, olive and grapeseed oil.

Another strategic way to brighten up your kitchen is by displaying tea. Store teabags in a pretty jar that says "tea." Or show off the beauty of tea leaves in glass jars. This will make your kitchen more cozy, and it will remind you to drink tea and therefore stay hydrated.

Changing the atmosphere of my kitchen has changed my attitude toward cooking immensely. My husband did an "overhaul" by opening up the kitchen to natural light: installing a small skylight, taking out part of a wall and removing dark window screens. We also had our cupboards "opened", by having the middle of each door panel replaced with glass, making the whole room seem both larger and cozier. Glass jars filled with dried goods and spices are the icing on the cake. With my favorite music playing on the computer, I sing, dance and cook. Thus, cooking has become less of a chore and more of an art, as it should be.

But before we add to our "Pantry", let's clean it out. Go through all your cupboards, fridge and freezer and get rid of everything unhealthy. I know this isn't always easy, so feel free to invite a good friend to help you. Don't worry that you're wasting food, because what you're throwing away isn't actually food at all, its garbage. And we all know garbage belongs in the trash. If it feels better you can donate it (not that needy people need junk food). It's a bigger waste to eat unhealthy foods or continue to waste space in your kitchen. We need a fresh start to fill our pantry with only real food. To check your old spices, rub some between your palms and smell, they should be aromatic. If not, it's time to give them the boot.

You have my permission: throw your unhealthy "food" away!

Shopping Tips

Someone recently asked me what I recommend be on a grocery list. I replied, "Besides fruit, nuts and seeds, all groceries should be ingredients to your week's recipes." And it's true. Although it may sound old-fashioned and remedial, weekly recipes are key to weight loss and health. Without recipes you don't know what to buy at the store, and without this information, you are bound to buy the wrong foods. Nor will you buy as many "right" ones.

Think about times you've set out for a new destination in your car with no map or number to call. You've wasted time, gas and needless energy because you didn't take a few minutes to plan your trip. This is exactly what happens when we go grocery shopping without a prepared list. Not only that, but you will probably find yourself making last minute trips to the store later that week, or even worse, eating take-out. Like an unplanned trip, unplanned grocery shopping is wasteful, stressful, and fattening.

The cookbook I use most is called Moosewood Restaurant Cooks at Home. The recipes are quick, easy, and delicious. In fact, my dinner guests often buy this cookbook the next day. One day each week (usually Sunday night), I choose five dinner recipes for the week and write them down. Then I list all the ingredients I need for my recipes, and viola – my grocery list (with additional fruit, nuts and seeds for snacks). When I shop, I simply stick to the list. I realize if I buy any junk food home, I'm bound to eat it, so the buck stops at the store.

Perhaps one of the most important things we can do to change our diet is to choose a better grocery store. When I find myself in a "typical" supermarket, I find it near impossible to find naturally high-fiber foods like fresh breads and organic produce. The legume selection is usually sparse, and everything seems to contain partially-hydrogenated oils and

MSG. There's lots of "food items" that don't seem to have any real food in them. I'm likely to bring home junk food, since it's everywhere I look. And sure, food might be cheap, but I'm getting what I pay for, which isn't much.

Yet when I shop at the natural foods co-op or other health food stores I can go crazy – and it's all good. The staff at the store has already done the work of selecting the best foods for me, and I no longer need to bring a magnifying glass to read ingredient labels. Nor do I have to look for the tiny little "health" or "organic" section of the store, since it's everywhere. I'm not tempted to buy junk food, since it doesn't exist. And even though prices might be higher, there is usually a bulk foods section where I find flour, grains and legumes at great prices. Besides, my health – and yours – is worth it.

A Restaurant Guide

Even though I am a firm advocate for homemade food, there is a time and place for restaurant dining. We just need a few primers.

Did you know that today's restaurant servings are two to three times as big as what restaurant servings were thirty years ago? Since the 1970s, the average plate size used in restaurants has increased by a radius of two inches. Plates used in the early 1900s were half the size of the plates we use today. If you live in a house built before the 1930's, you've probably noticed cupboard doors don't close while containing modern-day plates.

A typical meal at an ordinary American restaurant has one thousand calories—not including appetizer, drinks, or dessert. (The average restaurant meal in France is between one third and one half the size of ours.) Considering that most Americans today eat out for one third of their meals, that's a problem, especially for those of us who were raised to finish everything on our plates. (According the American Institute for Cancer Research, 67 percent of Americans eat everything on their plates, no matter how much is there.)

Why do restaurants eagerly give us all this extra food? People see bigger sizes as better value — more for their money. It makes us more likely to choose one eating establishment over another. Unfortunately, it is also making us fat.

Most of us have a hard time leaving food on our plates. We worry that we're wasting it. But excess food (no matter how healthy it is) is wasted whether it's thrown out or added to our waistlines. Contrary to what many of us learned as children, our becoming fatter is in no way going to help the hungry people of the world.

One more tip for restaurant eating: choose ethnic such as Italian, Mexican, Chinese, Japanese, Middle Eastern, or Thai over American/northern European. These restaurants offer more choices of meals without meat, and there are usually more whole grains and vegetables. For example, Italian restaurants usually offer meatless lasagna, and Middle Eastern restaurants almost always have falafel. Yum.

Mind-set

Eating out less often makes it more fun when you do. It becomes a treat, and you save money and calories.

When I do go out, I go with the expectation that I will most likely eat only half of my meal. I often bring a take-home box to the restaurant for a reminder. Sometimes I only order an appetizer or soup. When the waiter asks if I'd like something more, I reply, "Only if I'm still hungry. If I am I'll let you know."

Another healthy habit regarding food is getting used to saying, "No, thank you." That sounds easier than it is, but here's the trick: when we say no, we must understand that we are not missing out in any way. Nor are we denying ourselves something we want. In fact, it's just the opposite. We are being choosy. We're saying no, not because we can't eat or drink what's being offered, but because we don't want to. We don't want to be overweight, and we don't want to put junk into our precious bodies. Once we recognize that, we will be free to do what we truly want to do.

Another tip: stop making impulse decisions. Grocery stores put gum and candy in the checkout line strategically, hoping to entice you to buy on impulse. In fact, almost every time we say yes to the offer of food ("What would you like to start your meal with today?" or "Would you like anything to go with that?"), we are making an impulse decision. We are choosing food or drink out of compulsion or habit instead of hunger. We need to think critically, "Is this really what I want to eat? Is it that good, or should I hold out for something better?"

Ask yourself "Am I hungry?" Some of us haven't experienced real hunger in so long, we've forgotten the signs. Look for:

- stomach rumbling

- everything around you turns black when you stand up quickly

- you become shaky and/or moody

- you notice more saliva in your mouth (especially when you smell food)

We often go for food when we are bored, anxious, restless, or lonely. So when you find yourself looking for food, ask yourself what is really going on, and then address that issue. For example, if boredom leads you to the refrigerator, trade in the old habit of eating for a new one: making tea. Making tea gives you something to do, a nice warm mug to hold, and something to sip without the unnecessary calories.

Carolyn, my old roommate, played solitaire when she was bored or restless. Here are a few other ideas for dealing with loneliness or anxiety: call a friend, go for a short walk, draw, journal, or read a great book. Find something that comforts you in place of the false — and temporary — comfort of food.

Holiday Eating

Most people are stressed out by the holidays, in part due to weight gain. Let's reclaim our holidays, celebrating them by remembering sacred things and enjoying ourselves.

Most of us feel like we put on ten pounds during the holidays, but studies show the average American gains less than two pounds. So instead of stressing out about gaining weight, think of the holiday season as a reverse diet: a short period of eating differently than you do the rest of the year. When we get off a diet we gain back all our lost weight. The opposite is true of reverse diets. Once we revert to our normal eating patterns, we lose the extra holiday pounds. We really do.

If you find yourself stress-eating during this time of year, find other indulgences, like a bubble bath, a cup of tea by candlelight, a nature walk, prayer, or quiet music. And remember, exercise is the ultimate stress release, even when you feel sluggish.

Most of us feel guilty about overeating during the holidays and resolve to make drastic changes in our diet starting January. But let's stop that. Diet resolutions are often unrealistic, which sets us up for failure a few months (or weeks) later. Falling off the diet wagon makes us feel like a loser, and keeps us from real change. After all, if New Year's resolutions were successful year round, why make new ones every year?

The holidays are a great time to practice the "Do I really want that?" question. When surrounded by desserts and too much food, simply willing yourself not to eat will have the opposite effect. Instead, remind yourself that you can eat whatever you want, but you don't want just anything. Be picky and only eat the most delicious fare. And when you are tempted to eat, ask yourself if you're really hungry. If you are, eat slowly so you can stop when you're no longer hungry.

Here's another tip: eat before you go to a big meal. I know it sounds crazy, but hear me out. Most folks starve themselves all day before Thanksgiving or Christmas dinner. That's a Sumo Wrestler Diet. Remember that a little food in your belly throughout the day keeps you from overeating at meals. So whether you're off to a potluck or a holiday feast, eat a good high-fiber snack before you go. I usually find potluck food rather unappetizing, so I eat an entire meal before I leave the house, or plan on eating only from the dish I bring.

Now the good news. Some of the most common holiday foods are actually pretty high in fiber. My favorites are potatoes, sweet potatoes, cranberries, fruit salad, vegetables, and even pecan and pumpkin pie. Although mashed potatoes aren't likely to contain the skin, they still have some fiber, and some is better than none. Besides, potatoes have lots of other nutrients, including a good amount of vitamin C. Sweet potatoes have fiber as well as tons of carotenoids, which are antioxidants and precursors to vitamin A. You probably understand the value of cranberries, fruit salad, and vegetables, but pumpkin pie? Pumpkin is a squash, containing both fiber and carotenoids. Pecan pie is a great way to eat nuts, which are high in fiber and other nutrients. Sure, there's a lot of sugar in pie, but this is a holiday. Indulge a little!

The more fibrous food we eat during these festivities, the less likely we will be to overeat because we will be full.

Fiber satiates our appetite in myriad ways, making us fuller than other nutrients like starch or fat.

There are some foods I stay away from even during holidays: turkey, gravy, white biscuits, and any type of meat or sausage. Not only do these foods contain no fiber, they have few healthy nutrients and lots of dangerous fat. If you do eat some turkey, make it just enough to enjoy the taste so you don't feel deprived.

Alcohol intake needs to be closely monitored during the festive season. Alcohol contains many calories that don't make us full; it also causes us to overeat. It lowers our inhibitions to eat, and it over-stimulates our appetite so we eat when we're not hungry. Alcohol is also a diuretic, causing us to become dehydrated — and thus gain weight.

I'm not sure if anyone actually drinks eggnog, but you should know it's an extremely calorie-laden beverage. If you want something sweet, eat some dessert, don't drink it.

Workplace Food

What about all the junk food at the office year round? People are constantly being bombarded with donuts, muffins, and candy at their places of work. For some folks, giving treats is their "language of love." Find out who usually brings these goodies and ask if they could substitute or supplement by bringing roasted peanuts, almonds, pistachios, or fresh and/or dried fruit. Tell them you love and appreciate their offer of free munchies but you're trying to eat high-fiber foods. Not only would this likely help you, but many other people in the same situation. (If the donut-pushers don't respond favorably to your request, bring your own yummy healthy food so you're not tempted to eat the junk food.)

Love Your Food

Learn how to savor your food. In most cultures outside the US, people dedicate hours each day to purchase, grow, or gather food. Then they spend more hours preparing meals. They don't complain about the lengthy process but rather enjoy it. When they do eat, it's usually a social event with friends and family. Food is something to celebrate, not stress over. When these people dive into their meals, they take the time to really taste it. They eat slowly, enjoying the fragrance and flavor of each bite.

The word for "tasty" or "delicious" in Spanish is sabroso, which means "to savor." The root for this word is saber, meaning "to know." In order to know our food we need to taste it. And tasting takes time.

I'll never forget traveling in France. The French will sit at a restaurant for hours, talking, sipping wine, and savoring their food. It's like they have nothing better to do. And you know what? There might not be anything better to do than enjoying a delicious meal in good company.

Our bodies were designed to slowly savor the food we eat. Because nutrients give foods color, flavor, and aroma, the more nutritious our foods are, the more pleasing to our senses.

The longer food stays on our tongue, the more saliva our mouths secrete. Saliva coats food before it's sent down into the stomach. So the longer our food remains in our mouths before it's swallowed, the less likely we are to develop ulcers. Also, as we chew our food, the brain receives the message that we are becoming full. When we eat food slowly, we become truly satisfied, and we don't need to keep eating after we're no longer hungry.

What a contrast to the way most people in our country eat. We are often in a hurry, eating over the sink or in a car by ourselves. We hardly take the time to chew. It's no wonder ulcers are so common in the US. I sometimes wonder why we don't eat healthier foods if we hardly taste what we're eating anyway.

I have to admit I've struggled with my own dysfunctional relationship to food. As a nutritionist, I am committed to cooking healthy food from scratch. Yet this takes time. For years I cooked with a horrible attitude. Then one day I had an epiphany: how could I expect a healthy, delicious meal to not take time and energy? Beautiful things take time, and food is no exception. I chose to change my attitude and view my time in the kitchen as an art, not a chore.

My mother has learned the art of savoring food—especially desserts. She recognizes that desserts aren't worth eating if you don't take the time to taste them. So she almost always orders a dessert, though she rarely finishes eating one. "The first few bites taste the best, and I'm not still hungry at the end of my meal. I'm just eating it because I want something sweet after my dinner." You gotta love that woman.

When you go to a restaurant, make it a treat. Go somewhere that has low lighting, comfy seats, a quiet background, and scrumptious food. When you eat at home, try to eat with others as often as possible, and do your best to create a calm, enjoyable environment. Eat only food worth tasting; be choosy. Relax and savor each morsel. Give thanks for each bite, remembering that not everyone in the world has nearly as much food as you do.

13 LET'S GET MOVING

Many times when I speak on nutrition, people will ask me what I think about exercise. What kind of question is that? Honestly, how can a health professional deny the power of physical fitness in weight loss, longevity and overall wellness? So I usually answer that exercise is great, and we should all do it regularly. But of course everyone already knows that. They are looking for motivation. So even though you have heard exercise is necessary to live a long, healthy life a million times, let's revisit some of the best reasons for this claim. Then, let's work on developing an activity plan we can stick with.

Just as our bodies were designed for a high-fiber diet, they were designed for regular movement. Flexing our muscles, whether it be during a walk, run, dance or yoga class keeps our circulation moving – and it's all about circulation. That's because when our blood moves smoothly and quickly through our blood vessels it delivers vital oxygen and nutrients to each cell. If blood flow slows down, cells receive less oxygen and nutrients and will die prematurely. This makes us tired, because less oxygen is delivered to our brain. It also takes a toll on memory, mental clarity and concentration span.

Brain Boost

In other words, one great reason to be active is to keep your brain functioning properly. Studies show that people who exercise are far less likely to develop dementia and Alzheimer's disease. And for those of us who are younger, we simply won't be as sharp (or awake) as we could be. Studies also show exercise increases energy levels, improves sleep, memory, productivity, creativity, self-confidence and sexual satisfaction. Exercise also decreases anxiety and depression.

One study found that physical exercise lowered periodic leg movement levels in people who suffer from Restless Limb Syndrome, allowing them to sleep with fewer interruptions. Physical exercise increased sleep efficiency, rapid eye movement (REM) sleep, reduced wake after sleep onset, and reduced sleep latency.[1] Another study found that less that 50 minutes of walking on a treadmill a few hours before bedtime helps patients with insomnia get to sleep. Study participants who did moderate aerobic exercise in the evenings fell asleep more quickly, woke less often, and increased their total sleep time.[2]

The same circulation that improves blood flow to the brain also delivers loads of oxygen to our heart, preventing heart disease. The heart is a muscle, and stressing our heart physically makes it heart stronger and allows it to pump more blood to the rest of the body. Interestingly, our blood vessels (veins and arteries) are also made of muscle tissue, and therefore become more "elastic", or pliable, as circulation increases. This allows for yet better blood flow to cells, tissues and vital organs like our brain, heart... and reproductive organs.

That's right, exercise has been linked to a better sex life. After studying more than 31,000 men, the Harvard School of Public Health researchers reported that those who exercised regularly had a 30 percent lower risk for erectile dysfunction than the men with little or no physical activity.[3] Exercise also increases blood volume to the vaginal area, increasing sexual response in women.[4]

Speaking of improving the mood, regular physical activity has also been shown to combat depression. In treating mild to moderate depression one study found the effects of regular exercise had just as strong an affect as antidepressant medication. Depressive symptoms were reduced almost 50 percent in individuals who participated in 30-minute intensive aerobic exercise sessions three to five times a week. Even participants in the low-intensity aerobic exercise groups showed a 30 percent reduction in symptoms, and those who only did stretching exercises three days a week averaged a 29 percent decline.[5]

Studies also show that people who exercise are less likely to suffer from anxiety, and who doesn't need help chilling out these days? Since physical activity "stresses" our body, it releases neurotransmitters (chemicals in the brain and nervous system) that have calming effects, like dopamine and seratonin. One study found exercisers to be less anxious, depressed and neurotic, as well as more extraverted than non-exercisers.[6] Many of us turn to food, alcohol or other vices to relieve stress, but exercise is a healthy habit that has long-lasting effects on stress levels, and of course, helps us lose weight and live longer.

The same exercise-induced neurotransmitters help us to be more productive in the workplace, which indirectly reduces anxiety. People who exercise on work days are more productive, happier and suffer less stress than on non-gym days. University of Bristol researchers found that employees who enjoyed a workout before going to work, or during lunchbreaks, were better equipped to handle whatever the day threw at them. The study also found that people's general mood improved on days of exercise but became less calm on sedentary days. In particular, study participants found exercise helped them in time management, mental and interpersonal performance, managing workload, problem solving, concentration span, dealing calmly with stress, meeting deadlines and feeling motivated to work.[7]

Extra oxygen to the brain from exercise helps us beat fatigue, especially for those of us who are sedentary. One study found non-exercisers who suffered chronic fatigue were able to increase their energy levels by 20 percent and decrease their fatigue by 65 percent by engaging in regular, low intensity exercise.[8] So even though physical activity is probably the last thing you want to do when you're tired, ultimately, it will help you feel less tired less often.

Have you ever noticed that during a time of physical exertion you had a brilliant idea? That's because your brain is on drugs – healthy, naturally occurring drugs called endorphins. Endorphins are natural pain relievers our bodies produce when we exercise, and they are chemically similar to morphine. The combination of increased brain oxygen, endorphins and other neurotransmitters work to give us what is known as a "runner's high". This high often results in mental clarity and even "epiphanies" where we come up with new ideas or solutions to a problem. It also can result in feelings of self-confidence and empowerment: a feeling as though you can "conquer the world".

I have personally experienced exercise-induced "highs" countless times while hiking, running or biking. I'll often return home with a new outlook, idea or both (although taking the time to write ideas down is another matter). And I'm not the only one: it's not uncommon for creative people to use bodily movement to overcome "blocks". Studies show that creative thinking scores are significantly higher after a bout of exercise.[9]

If all these benefits weren't enough, new research indicates that exercise actually builds new brain cells. Now who couldn't benefit from a bigger brain? Exercise boosts brainpower by building new brain cells in a brain region linked with memory and memory loss. Tests on mice showed they grew new brain cells in a brain region called the dentate gyrus, a part of the brain that is known to be affected in the age-related memory decline that begins around age 30 in humans. Researchers used magnetic resonance imaging scans to help document the process in mice – and then used MRIs to look at the brains of people before and after exercise. They found the same patterns, which suggests that people also grow new brain cells when they exercise.

Those same brain cells generated by exercise today will keep our memory more sharp in our older years. That means we are at less risk for dementia and Alzheimer's. In a study of more than 1,400 adults, those who were physically active during middle age were 52% less likely to develop dementia 21 years later than their sedentary counterparts. The exercisers' chance of developing Alzheimer's disease was slashed by 62% overall. These patterns were even stronger in people with the ApoE e4 gene, which is associated with higher risk of developing Alzheimer's disease.[10] How incredible to think the time we take to stay fit today is an investment that reaps dividends for years to come. Our golden years can be a time of joy, not confusion.

Dierdre's story

Perhaps the best reason to exercise is it can give us a sense of control over our chaotic lives. Workouts can be therapeutic. My friend Dierdre started running at age 55, which allowed her to deal with stress and trauma in a way that nothing else could. In her own words, she tells her story:

I started running because life was chasing me, relentlessly, mercilessly, and running seemed like a good way to get out of its steamroller path. I was training for endurance — I needed piles of it to get through my life's dizzying onslaught. One death. Another. Another. A nest newly emptied, still emptying. Moving. Remodeling three houses on two coasts, emptying, repairing. Estate documents. Wills. The divorce had bogged down, my life as I knew it had ended, and I was running to leave all that behind.

My son Alex, a rock climber, is to blame. He runs to keep in shape on non-climbing days, and his take on it has always been, "If you can do a mile and a half, you can do two. If you can do two, you can do three."

He's a successful athlete, so I believed him – even though the first day that Juno, our malamute, set out with me for our first jog, I could hardly manage a mile (Juno could have kept going a lot farther).

Alex ran my first 10K with me, running backwards and in circles around me, amusing me with stories about his recent trip to Spain, as I labored to suck in air and to convince my feet to keep moving.

But running is directional. You can run in a loop, straight out and back, from point A to point B – but you're always going somewhere. Where was I going?

My first conclusion was obvious: away. Escape sounded like a no-brainer. Each time I headed out the door, I could forget all the emotional pain, the frustration, the wasted years, the unending morass of paperwork. My footfall was hypnotic. It was another world, a tidy one that made sense and followed strict rules.

But life has its own rules. The ink wasn't dry on the divorce before a faulty heart ended my newly-ex-husband's life. My elderly father died, too, my last parent, which left a gaping hole in my family as I knew it. Now, besides all the houses I had to deal with, the executorship and all the financial stuff I knew nothing about, and the full-time job, I also had kids who had just lost their Dad.

So I kept running. Running is balance, and in my out-of-balance life it was something I could control. I made charts. I ran on a schedule. I got a little better, a little faster, and began having to leave the exhausted, old dog at home. I ran races — 5Ks, 10Ks, 12Ks, half-marathons, whatever the region offered. I scheduled them into my new, weird life, around the lawyers and financial advisors and long-distance calls and endless paperwork.

I found out about the marathon, and scheduled that in, even though handling several estates while working full-time seemed to take every waking moment. It clearly wasn't the time for this. My son had a horrible near-death brush with a pile of rocks at eight thousand feet in a winter storm, and we got acquainted with the trauma center. My good friend died in a freak accident. My dog died. A lifelong friend's twenty-year-old son took his own life. In between, numb, I ran.

Tying my running shoes became a symbolic act. I was girding myself against life. With those shoes, I could do anything. I had never met anyone who'd run a marathon, never known any serious runners besides my daughter, who ran her first marathon the same year I ran mine. It certainly wasn't something that I, in any sane, rational moment, would ever undertake. Weak lungs, structural body defects, all kinds of strikes against me seemed to make it impossible. And yet, I never questioned it. I would tie on my shoes, and life was reduced to an orderly, soothing sameness. Never once before the marathon did I question why I did it.

At about mile three of my first, the California International Marathon, I began to suffocate. I immediately thought of my lifelong *irregular heart -- and then I realized I just wasn't sucking in enough air around the tears. They poured down my throat, my face, a complete surprise.*

As I pounded out the mindless rhythm and struggled to keep breathing and putting one foot in front of the other, bits of things I'd read about grieving and mourning flashed through my mind. True, I'd never had time for either.

But this couldn't be for that, I knew it. And besides, what did that have to do with running?

A few miles farther, I felt something oddly familiar about the wide avenue we were on. I'd read about the marathon route a million times, and knew the name of the road. Could this be the same street I always took to go shopping, to the bank, to work? It looked different. It took a few more miles before it struck me: without cars, filled only with people and their soft footfalls, the busy, trafffic-filled road I knew had been transformed. The trees that lined it swooshed in the breeze, and offered a birdsong background for the heavy breathing and cheers that surrounded me.

Running clearly changed everything. The past was over, and I knew that this road, like my life, would never look the same again.

The tears disappeared as I neared the half-marathon point. After that, I began to recognize the topography, the familiar scenery. It looked different, but I still knew it.

And I knew my tears, now, too. They weren't for the past, exactly; they were a good-bye to that past. Change is hard. But I had my running shoes, firmly tied.

People who knew me before, non-runners, said to me, after the marathon, "Okay, you've proven that you can do it. You can stop now." Which, I guess, makes sense to them. They don't realize that I'm on my way to a new life -- and the only way to get there is to run.

Let's sum up some of the amazing outcomes of regular exercise:

- *Better sleep*
- *Improves sex life*
- *Relieves depression*
- *Reduces anxiety*
- *Improves productivity*
- *Combats fatigue*
- *Increases creativity*
- *Grows new brain cells*
- *Protects against memory loss, dementia and Alzheimer's*
- *Inexpensive therapy*

Social Capital

Just as our bodies are designed for movement, our souls are inherently social. Even the most introverted among us needs supportive relationships, and our exercise rituals can help provide the social support we need. This will help reinforce our commitment to fitness as well as provide other life-sustaining benefits, like a sense of community.

Social networks are vital to our physical and mental health. Most of us know that friendships and positive relationships help prevent depression, but did you know they help prevent premature death? That's because healthy social interaction improves our immune system, which means we are less likely do die of cancer as well as catch a cold. So to improve our health, we need friends.

One study tracked 629 older women for almost six years, analyzing their social networks and incidence of stroke. After adjusting for confounding factors, researchers found isolated women experienced strokes at greater than twice the rate of those with more social relationships. In fact, the connection between isolation and stroke were so pronounced that the study authors concluded that, "the magnitude of the association rivals that of conventional risk factors". In other words, isolation was as much a risk factor for stroke as smoking, high blood pressure and high cholesterol.[11]

Another study followed over 2700 elderly people for 13 years, looking for the overlap between social activity and overall mortality. The study found those who were most socially active were eighty percent more likely to survive compared to those who were had the least social interaction. In fact, the social factor was just as strong a predictor for survival as the exercise factor.[12]

Research shows that social "capital" (or positive relationships) increases physical and emotional health more than other factors, such as socio-economic status, age, and income.[13]

So here are some tips for creating a social exercise environment from longevity guide, Mark Stibich, P.H.D.

- **Play a Sport**: Joining a team sport is a great way to meet people and bond with them. Team sports lead to great stories and social interaction. From bowling to rugby, a team sport will have you meet and working together with 10 or more other people. Team sports also will have you committing to a whole season of exercise and physical activity. Pick a sport that's right for you, check out local community centers and find yourself a team to play for.

- **Find a Buddy**: Exercising with another person can help motivate you and make your workouts more interesting. Find someone who is dependable and you like to be with to go to the gym together, run on weekends with or go out for a bike ride with.

- **Exercise for Charity**: 5Ks, bike rides and other events are great fundraisers for charity. You'll meet hundreds of people, get some exercise and raise some money for a good cause. Once you get into the world of charity fundraisers, you'll be amazed how many people you meet.

- **Join a Class**: Group fitness classes are also a great way to meet people and add a social element to your workout. Find a class that you enjoy, and show up a little early. Ask questions of the people there and get advice on how to do some of the exercises. You'll be looking forward to your exchanges with other classmates and with the instructor.

Personally, I don't know where I'd be without my "fitness community". Two nights a week I join a dozen or so other people at the local rock-climbing gym for a time of strenuous activity and cavorting. I look forward not only to releasing stress physically, but mentally and emotionally as I enter a refreshing change of scenery, surrounded by new friends and acquaintances. We know we need one another for climbing purposes, but we also need one another socially. And exercise is what brings us together.

Exercise as Opportunity

Aside from the double-benefits of social and physical activity, exercise also allows us opportunities to improve our health in other unique ways, such as listening to music and spending time outdoors. Both music and nature have the ability to give us transcendent experiences, where we feel like we've temporarily left our mundane circumstances and mental processes. This, coupled alongside the additional oxygen flow to the brain and endorphins from exercise, can cause our mental state to change from feeling trapped in a rut, to an escape of beauty and serenity. Aside from the fact that feelings of transcendence improve our immune function, who doesn't need to escape from a rut these days?

One of the ways music works is by engaging the frontal lobe of the brain, since the brain has to sort out tones, timing and sequencing of various sounds, to comprehend music. The frontal lobe is the part of the brain associated with higher mental functions, like abstract thinking. One study tested 33 men and women during the final weeks of a cardiac rehabilitation program. Each of the participants were tested for mental performance after exercising without music, and exercising with music. On average, the participants performed more than twice as well on a verbal fluency test after listening to music while exercising than they did after exercising without the music.[14]

Music has also been shown to fight depression and chronic pain. In one study, researchers randomly assigned chronic pain sufferers to one of three groups. The first group and second groups listened to music selected by researchers or of their own choosing, while the third group did not listen to any music. Both the music groups experienced less pain and depression than the control group.[15] A similar study found music helped to lesson anxiety in psychiatric patients.[16]

According to Daniel Levitin, author of *This is Your Brain on Music: The Science of a Human Obsession*, music is wired to the movement related areas of the brain. That part, the motor cortex, is the same part of the brain that helps us move in a willful way, for example, to jog or dance. "When music hits our eardrums, part of the signal flows up toward the motor cortex and creates a connection."[17] Music and movement work synergistically, and music plays a powerful role in getting and keeping us moving.

Brunel University's School of Sport and Education in England found that carefully selected music can significantly increase a person's physical endurance and make the experience of aerobic exercise far more positive. In the study, thirty participants exercised on a treadmill while listening to a selection of motivational rock or pop music. They were asked to keep in strict time with the beat. The findings show that music can enhance endurance by 15% and improve the 'feeling states' of exercisers, helping them to derive much greater pleasure from the task. Researchers even found that music helped exercisers feel more positive when pushing themselves to their physical limits.[18]

Along with music, exercise gives us an opportunity to get outside. Studies are finding benefits to spending time outdoors. Increasingly, we are realizing how imperative fresh air, sunlight and nature are for mental and emotional health. Being out during the day allows our bodies to produce vitamin D, a nutrient well known for its role in bone density and immunity. Vitamin D is widely deficient throughout the U.S., in large part due to lack of outdoor activity. Exposure to natural sunlight has been associated with improvement in mood, reduced mortality among patients with cancer, and reduced length of hospitalization for patients who have experienced heart attacks.[19]

One study compared hospital patients' recovery time and sunlight exposure. They compared those housed on the "bright" or "dim" side of the same hospital unit. Researchers found patients who stayed on the bright side of the hospital experienced less perceived stress, less pain, and took 22% less analgesic medication per hour regardless of age.[20] Similarly, another hospital-based study found that patients placed in rooms with a window view of a natural setting (including trees and greenery) recovered faster than those who did not.[21]

Nature plays such an effective role combating depression, it even has it's own name: ecotherapy. Researchers from the University of Essex compared the benefits of a 30-minute walk in a country park with a walk in an indoor shopping mall on a group of people suffering from depression. After the country walk, 71 percent reported decreased levels of depression and stress while 90 percent reported increased feelings of self-esteem. In contrast, only 45 percent experienced a decrease in depression after walking in the mall.[22] Researchers then conducted a second study, asking 108 people with various mental health problems about their experiences in nature. A whopping 94 percent of participants responded that being in nature lifted depression while 90 percent said the combination of nature and exercise had the greatest effect.[23]

If sunlight and nature have healing, stress and pain-relieving properties, we can not doubt their protective effects on health. And we need to make sure we receive a regular dose of both.

Although I don't particularly enjoy running, I have found that music and nature help me keep going when I'm ready to stop (usually about five minutes after I've begun). Seeing the moon at dusk, or running around a tree-filled park gives me a feeling of relaxation and release. Music provides an impetus to move and keep moving. I feel better and have more energy for several hours after running. If you're like me, you will find exercise much more enjoyable – and perhaps possible – with these environmental conditions.

Back to Basics

Perhaps one of the worst things that happens as we grow up is we forget to play. Our society has become so obsessed with profit (or things that lead to profit, such as education) and entertainment that we've even forgotten children need to play more than sit in school. Creative physical activity refreshes us mentally and rewires our brains, as opposed to passively sticking to a routine.

One way we can keep things fresh is to change exercise with the seasons. This has the added benefit of keeping us outdoors. For example, in the summer months I love to kayak. Kayaking not only gives me a wonderful upper-body workout, but the ability to actually enjoy the summer heat, since I can cool off in the water anytime. It also brings me to scenic landscapes I wouldn't ordinarily enjoy.

In the winter months when daylight hours are limited, I climb at the local rock climbing gym. Climbing also provides a unique workout because it engages the mind as well as the body, and it is social, since climbers need a belay partner.

In the spring and fall, I try to exercise outdoors as much as possible to enjoy the beauty and temperature of the season. For me this means mountain biking (biking on dirt trails in a wooded area — carefully), hiking, as well as walking and running. Mountain biking is my all-time favorite activity, since it provides a complete change of scenery (trees, mountains and open spaces) and is faster paced than hiking.

Obviously, I really am very committed to exercise. But for those who are lesser so, playfulness can mean a simple change of location or routine. For example, if you like to walk, try walking around a different park or through a different neighborhood – even if it requires driving to get there. On weekends, try walking on trails, also known as hiking. Trail walking provides beautiful scenery and keeps things new. And of course, adding music to your walk will make it even more enjoyable and stimulating.

Another way to spice things up is to use your body for transportation. Walking or biking to run errands might require more preparation, but well worth it whenever possible. Find the safest, most scenic route to your destination, and give it a go. Consider biking to work at least once a week. Bicycle commuting gets us outdoors, wakes us up, and keeps us in shape – and we don't have to deal with traffic.

One of the reasons Europeans are believed to be less overweight than Americans is because they walk much more than we do. But they usually walk with an intention to arrive at a location, not for the sake of exercise. This is also true for bicycle riding. When we walk or ride to arrive at a location, it seems less like "exercise" and is likely to become a regular part of our daily or weekly routine.

I realize cities in Europe are much more compact and "walkable" than those in the U.S. Living in the suburbs makes it difficult to get anywhere on foot or by bike. One of the reasons my husband and I chose to live in the downtown region of our city was so we could drive less and conversely, walk and bike more. We have lived all 15 years of our married life with only one car, my husband and I both biking to work and most errands. The last five years have included walking or biking with our daughter, and it's been wonderful. We all stay in better shape, and save money on gas and car maintenance.

If you live in a place too remote to leave the car at home, you might want to consider moving to a more walkable area. I know that's asking a lot, but it would radically improve your physical, mental and emotional health. Imagine living in a region with tree-lined streets: you would want to walk and you'd experience "ecotherapy" to boot. Or living within walking (or biking) distance of shops, cafés and restaurants. You would become much more active, and you would likely enlarge your circle of aquaintances, or "social capital".

Living in a walkable community is so important that some health psychologists are collaborating with urban planners to get more people on their feet and out of their cars. According to a study in the American Journal of Health Promotion, people who live in high sprawl areas, relying on cars for all their transportation needs, weigh more than people who live in compact cities. For example, a person living in the study's most sprawling county – Geauga County, Ohio – weighed, on average, six pounds more and walked 79 minutes less each month than people living in the study's most compact area of New York County. In addition, sprawling county residents were more likely to suffer from high blood pressure.[24]

Researcher James Sallis, PhD, a psychology professor at San Diego State University, says he is alarmed at the impact sprawling cities can have on people's health. "Since the 1940s, we have been building our cities for cars and not for walking," says Sallis, an expert in physical activity interventions. "So we've gotten to the point in our suburbs where we can't walk anywhere."

Dr. Sallis' research found that residents living in neighborhoods with higher density and connectivity as well as with more shops and homes mixed together walk 15 to 30 minutes more per week than residents who live in sprawling communities.[25] Interestingly, cities rated " most fit" by the American College of Sports Medicine tend to also be the most walkable.

Why should Europeans have all the fun – and better health? We all could benefit from a lifestyle where walking (or biking) is part of the normal routine. So what if it costs a little more to live in a walkable neighborhood? Sickness and health care cost a lot more.

And while I'm making outlandish suggestions, here's another one that will have enormous benefits for your entire being: if possible, work less. Not only are Americans unique in living far from where we work and shop, we also spend more hours working (and commuting to work) than any other country. In addition, work hours increase almost every year, according to a study by CNN.[26]

Of course the more time we spend working, the less time for play. And when we do play, we tend to find ourselves so exhausted, we sit passively in front of a screen. Yet some of us can buck the system. We can make choices to live on a smaller income with the benefit of more free time – and better health. If that sounds ludicrous, think how ludicrous it is living in a culture where money is esteemed more than mental, emotional and physical health. Or that most developed countries work fewer hours, make less money, and have better health than we do. It's not so much a decision to be counter-culture as it is to turn back the clock to a time when one's quality of life mattered more than one's income.

Just as my husband and I decided to live with only one car, we also decided I would never work full-time, unless absolutely necessary. This has allowed us to eat meals made from scratch, shop farmer's markets and garden, thus saving money, as well as leading more creative, less hurried lives. Of course, it has also allowed me to spend time raising our daughter, never mind the money saved from daycare. We are less stressed than most people our age, and we have more time to be physically active.

And it's not just me. Research shows that a flexible work life, including telecommuting and job shares, is good for our health. A study at Wake Forest University School of Medicine found that if people have the ability to work from home and to compress work weeks, they are more likely to make healthier lifestyle choices, to exercise more and to sleep better. The health benefits are believed to be from a more flexible schedule allowing for more time for exercise and time management.[27]

Nor is it shocking that working overtime wreaks havoc on our health. One study in Norway compared 1350 people working overtime with almost 9,000 people who did not work overtime. Researchers found both male and female overtime workers to have significantly higher anxiety and depressive disorders compared with those who worked normal hours.[28] A study published in the International Journal of Obesity found body mass (BMI) to be higher in people who spent fewer hours sleeping and more hours working.[29]

So for your health, work less and play more. Exercise doesn't need to be drudgery. Make workouts true "play" that break up the monotony of daily life: get outside, be social and listen to great music.

PART TWO: Recipes and Meal Plan

Meet the Chef

No healthy-eating book would be complete without recipes and a meal plan. And since I happen to know one of the best meal planners in the world, I thought I'd share her with you. Allow me to introduce my friend Jennifer Brewer. Or better yet, I'll have her introduce herself...

Hi, I'm Jennifer. Like Bronwyn, I too am a weight loss expert. This isn't something I studied in school but acquired through personal experience. I went on my first diet at age 13. I can still remember the feeling of watching my classmates eat their bags of chips and chocolate cupcakes, wondering why I had to be the heavy one. Why did I have to feel hungry all the time?

Of course, the diets I subjected myself to were ridiculous (grapefruit, cabbage soup, you name it) and I could never stick to them very long. My teens and twenties are a blur of carrot sticks, cottage cheese, melba rounds and jeans that wouldn't quite fit. I yo-yoed up and down so often and gained and lost the same 30 pounds 10 different times in my life. Yes, that is 300 lbs! Wow! Oprah calls her fat years her "unconscious" years, and this was exactly how this time felt for me—like I was living someone else's life.

So, what is someone with major food issues going to study in college? Nutrition, of course! Thinking that the right amount of knowledge would surely heal my food issues, I received both my Bachelors and Masters degrees in human nutrition. Yes, I knew all about fats, carbohydrates and proteins, but I still didn't know how to turn off the voice telling me to buy the big bag of tortilla chips because I deserved them and then chastising me for not having the self-control to stop eating them. There wasn't a class for that!

After graduation, I started working with college students on improving their diet and many of them had food-related issues. So, here I was, trying to help them improve their health with diet, yet I myself was still obsessed with food and dieting. I was at a low point in my ever yo-yoing weight so I looked the part, but inside I was struggling.

So, what is a Nutritionist with food issues who feels like a big fraud going to do next? Go to Culinary School and become a Chef, of course! Fortunately, I attended the Natural Gourmet Culinary School in NYC, a culinary school focused on whole, natural foods cooking. I loved learning about foods that nourished me physically and actually tasted good (unlike cottage cheese and cardboard crackers).

I really started to look at food differently. Food lost it's "Good/Bad", "On My Diet/Off My Diet" status and became just food, and delicious food at that! In fact, I couldn't believe how delicious healthy food could be when prepared the right way.

During this time in culinary school, I ate as much as I needed without portioning foods or counting calories. Interestingly, my weight started to stabilize without me focusing on it. More important than the way I looked on the outside was the way the voices started to quiet down. Even though I was surrounded by food, I was thinking about it less and less.

What also came during this time was an acceptance of who I am and the foods I love. One of my favorite go-to diets in my early years was the low carb diet, mainly because it worked so well for me (it eliminated like 75% of what I would typically eat—I love carbs!). I could lose weight like crazy on that diet. But, I was seriously neglecting the inner child part of me that loves bread and starch. Now I realize that I just can't eliminate an entire group of foods that I love and expect to feel peaceful about it. And I also know that I feel better when I choose carbohydrates that are whole and minimally processed.

I want to acknowledge you for having the courage to try a new way of eating! I truly believe that when we eat simple, unprocessed plant foods we nourish ourselves way beyond fat, carbohydrates, protein or calories. By filling up on pure foods loaded with fiber and nutrition, we can stop counting calories and start actually living our lives. And by making our healthy foods taste amazing, we honor our inner child who still wants that yum-yum feeling.

Jennifer's Note About Recipes

These recipes include some of my all-time favorites. Please think of them as templates, not set in stone. Choose recipes that can be duplicated with different ingredients over and over again. For example, when you find a really good bean soup, think about how you could use different beans and spices to give it a different flavor the next time you prepare it. Other examples of good recipe templates are curries, stir-fries and stews. To save time, most of my recipes include vegetables, proteins and grains all in the same dish (one-pots rock!). You will save valuable time because you won't have to prepare 2-3 different side dishes and there will be fewer dishes to do.

Most of my recipes call for sautéing the ingredients in high-quality oil (like olive or coconut) as the first step in the recipe. Use a good quality, unrefined oil for this step and add the seasonings at this point as well, since dried herbs and spices release more of their flavor in warm oil.

I recommend sea salt in all of my recipes, which is less refined. I will typically say "Add salt and pepper to taste" so the amount you add is up to you. I call for tamari (soy sauce) in recipes quite often, so if you are concerned about salt, I recommend purchasing reduced sodium soy sauce. Also, you cannot match the flavor of using vegetable broth in your soups and stews. You can substitute water, but you will need to add more seasonings if you do. If you make a very flavorful broth, you might not need to add as much seasoning to the actual soup. You can either make your own broth (wonderful!) or purchase vegetable broth that has already been prepared.

When making recipes with dry beans, add salt at the end of cooking. Salt slows down the cooking of beans so it is best not to add it until the end. Remember: add salt and other seasonings gradually. You can always add more but can't take it out if you add too much. Add acidic foods at the end of cooking. Acidic foods like vinegar and lemon juice will enhance flavors and might be just what your recipe needs to make it taste just right.

Have fun making these delicious and healthy recipes! Experiment with your own favorite beans, vegetables and flavors. This time is about trying new things, learning new things and deciding what will work for your lifestyle.

Eat Well, Be Well and LOVE Every Bite!

~Jennifer Brewer

www.nourishingnutrition.com

Breakfast Recipes

Comforting Quinoa Breakfast Cereal

Serves 4

Instead of sugary cereal breakfast, try this high protein treat. Quinoa (pronounced keen-wa) is a gluten-free whole grain that is a great source of protein and minerals like calcium and iron and several of the B vitamins. This recipe is an easy way to get complex carbohydrates and protein at the same meal, and it is delicious!

2 ½ cups milk, soymilk or almond milk

1 cup yellow quinoa, rinsed

1 apple, cored and diced

½ cup raisins

1 Tablespoon agave nectar, honey or maple syrup

1 teaspoon cinnamon

½ cup walnuts (sprinkled on at the end)

Bring milk and a pinch of salt to a light boil. Stir in quinoa and diced apples, reduce heat to low and simmer until quinoa is tender, about 15-20 minutes. Remove from heat and stir in raisins, sweetener and cinnamon. Sprinkle with walnuts and top with extra milk if desired. If you have leftovers, gently heat with extra milk the next morning and serve!

Spinach Tofu Frittata with a Potato Crust

Serves 6

2 Yukon gold potatoes, sliced thinly

1 pound firm tofu, crumbled

½ cup unsweetened soy or almond milk

¼ teaspoon turmeric

2 teaspoons Dijon mustard

2 Tablespoons all purpose flour

Salt and freshly–ground black pepper

1 Tablespoon olive oil

2 garlic cloves, minced

1 yellow onion, diced

1 red pepper, diced

½ teaspoon dried thyme

2 cups baby spinach leaves

Preheat the oven to 350 degrees. Peel and slice the potatoes thinly. Grease an 8 x 11 casserole dish. Arrange sliced potatoes in the bottom of the pan, overlapping, and bake for 15 minutes. Remove and set aside.

Place the tofu in a food processor, along with the milk, turmeric, mustard, flour, and a sprinkle of salt and pepper. Process until smooth and set aside.

Heat the oil in a large skillet over medium heat. Add the garlic, onion, pepper and thyme and cook until onion is clear, about 5 minutes.

Place spinach leaves over the potato crust. Place tofu mixture and red pepper mixture into the dish, spreading over the spinach (and combining in the process).

Bake for 25-30 minutes or until firm.

Salads and Spreads
White Bean Guacamole

Serves 4

Holy Guacamole---fiber, fiber, fiber! By adding a can of white beans to traditional guacamole you get all the deliciousness of creamy avocados with a healthy dose of protein and fiber. This way, you get full long before you eat the entire bowl of guacamole!

2 ripe avocados, flesh removed

1 can white beans, drained and rinsed well

2 plum tomatoes, diced

juice from 1–2 limes

salt and pepper to taste

½ small red onion, diced

½ cup fresh cilantro, minced

Place avocado flesh and white beans into a bowl and mash together well using a potato masher or fork. Add remaining ingredients, seasoning to taste and serve.

Lentil Salad

Serves 4

Lentils are loaded with fiber and protein, keep you full and provide sustained energy. Use canned to save time or cook your own from dry.

2–15 oz cans lentils or, 2 cups cooked from dry

¼ cup olive oil

2 Tablespoons apple cider vinegar

1 Tablespoon Dijon mustard

½ small red onion, minced

½ cup chopped fresh parsley

2 Tablespoons fresh chopped thyme

Sea salt and pepper to taste

Mix together the olive oil, vinegar, mustard, red onion, parsley and thyme, whisk well, and season to taste with salt and pepper. Stir in lentils and refrigerate until service.

Savory Red Lentil Pate

Serves 4-6

1 cup red lentils

2 cups water or vegetable stock

2 Tablespoons coconut oil

3 cloves garlic, minced

1 large onion, chopped fine

1 teaspoon dried thyme

1 teaspoon salt

½ cup minced parsley

½ teaspoon black pepper

1 teaspoon apple cider vinegar

Place lentils into a saucepan with the water or stock, bring to a boil, reduce heat to medium and simmer, covered, for 20 minutes. In a large skillet, heat the oil. Add the garlic, onions and herbs and saute over medium heat, stirring constantly, for about 10 minutes, or until the onions and garlic are browned and fragrant. When the lentils are done, mash them thoroughly with a fork or potato masher, then add the onion mixture and parsley. Season to taste with salt vinegar and pepper.

Forbidden Rice Salad

Serves 4

The best way to make a grain salad is when the grain is COLD, so prepare the rice in advance.

2 cups cooked black or forbidden rice

½ cup almonds, chopped

½ cup chopped parsley

2 stalks celery, chopped

½ bunch scallions, chopped

Dressing:

¼ cup olive oil

2 Tablespoons brown rice vinegar

Salt and black pepper to taste

Combine all the ingredients for the dressing. Right before serving, toss the rice with the almonds, parsley, celery and scallions. Drizzle with the dressing and serve at once.

Kale and Tahini Salad

Serves 4

Try this salad for lunch or for your 3:00 snack! Raw foods increase our vitality and can help battle that dreaded afternoon slump. Tahini is sesame seed paste and it is a good source of calcium, plus it makes things creamy and delish!

Nutrition All Star: Miso is a fermented soybean paste that contains beneficial enzymes, aiding digestion.

1 head lacinato or dinosaur kale, thinly sliced

sea salt

1 clove garlic, minced

¼ cup tahini

1 Tablespoon miso

¼ cup water

2 Tablespoons lemon juice

1 plum tomato, diced

1 green onion, sliced

Place sliced kale in a bowl, sprinkle with sea salt and "massage" for 3 minutes until kale starts to break down. In a bowl with a whisk or food processor, mix together garlic, tahini, miso, water and lemon juice. Stir tahini sauce into kale and add tomato and green onion. Refrigerate until ready to eat.

Soups and Stews
Baby Lima Bean Soup with Chard

Serves 6

2 cups dried baby lima beans (small white beans) soaked overnight**

2 Tablespoons olive oil

1 onion, chopped

2 cloves garlic, minced

2 carrots, sliced

2 celery stalks, diced

2 bay leaves

1 strip kombu (sea vegetable)

1 teaspoon dried thyme

½ teaspoon smoked paprika

4 cups vegetable stock

4 cups water

1 bunch green swiss chard, thinly sliced

1 teaspoon apple cider vinegar

Salt and pepper, to taste

**Soak the dried beans in enough water to cover overnight. Drain beans and rinse a few times with fresh water (this takes the gas producing stuff off). Set aside.

Warm olive oil in a large soup pot over medium heat and add onion, garlic, carrots, celery, and spices. Cook, stirring occasionally, for about 5 minutes, until onion is clear. Add soaked beans, kombu, vegetable stock and water. Bring to a boil, then reduce heat and simmer, covered for 45-55 minutes, until beans are slightly tender.

Now, add sliced chard. Simmer for another 15 minutes, or until beans are tender. Add the vinegar and salt and pepper to taste, remove bay leaves and kombu strip and serve.

Sweet Potato and Black Bean Chili

Serves 6-8

1 Tablespoon olive oil

1 medium red onion, chopped

1 Anaheim pepper, chopped

2 cloves garlic, minced

2 sweet potatoes (1½ lbs), peeled and cut into ½ -inch cubes

1 28-ounce can whole plum tomatoes

1 cup water or vegetable stock

2 15-ounce cans black beans, drained or 3 cups cooked black beans

1 dried chipotle pepper (smoked jalepeno), seeded and chopped (easiest to do with scissors)

1 teaspoon cumin

1 teaspoon chili powder

½ cup chopped fresh cilantro leaves

Warm the oil in a large pan over medium heat and add the onion, pepper, garlic, and sweet potato chunks. Saute, stirring often, until onions are soft, about 5 minutes.

Add the tomatoes, breaking them up with the back of a wooden spoon. Add water or stock, beans, chipotle, cumin, and chili powder, bring to boil, reduce heat to simmer, cover, and cook for 30 minutes, or until sweet potatoes are tender. Stir in cilantro and serve.

Shiitake Mushroom Miso Soup

Serves 6

Nutrition All-Star: Miso is a fermented soy product, rich in beneficial enzymes. The good qualities are destroyed by heat, so it is added at the end of cooking and should not be boiled.

1 oz dried shiitake mushrooms

2 cups water

2 teaspoons olive oil

1 large leek, chopped

1 large carrot, sliced

2 stalks celery, chopped

¼ cup chopped fresh sage (or 1 tsp. dried)

½ teaspoon dried thyme

1 15-oz can cannellini beans or other white beans, drained

3 cups vegetable broth

salt and black pepper to taste

½ cup vegetable broth

1 Tablespoon light miso

2 cups baby spinach leaves

Combine mushrooms and water in a saucepan; cover and simmer for 15 minutes. Drain mushrooms in a colander over a bowl, reserving liquid. When cool enough to handle, thinly slice and set aside.

Heat oil in a large soup pot over medium-high heat. Add leek, carrot, celery, and mushrooms to pan; sauté 5 minutes or until tender. Add sage and thyme and cook for another 2 minutes.

Add the beans, 3 cups vegetable broth, and reserved mushroom liquid and bring to a boil. Cover, reduce heat, and simmer 10 minutes. Right before serving, stir in spinach leaves until just wilted. Also, whisk miso into ½ cup vegetable broth and stir mixture into the soup. DO NOT boil it after adding miso. Add salt and pepper to taste and serve.

Chana Dal Soup

Serves 6

Chana Dal are baby chickpeas, very cute indeed! If you can't find them, you could substitute yellow split peas.

1 Tablespoon coconut oil

1 large leek, washed well and sliced

2 stalks celery, sliced

2 carrots, sliced

3 cloves garlic, minced

1 cup dry chana dal (baby chickpeas) or yellow split peas

1 strip kombu

2½ cups vegetable stock

2½ cups water

1 15-oz can coconut milk

½ teaspoon Thai chili paste**

1 Tablespoon fresh squeezed lemon juice

salt and pepper to taste

3 cups baby spinach leaves, washed

Melt oil in a large saucepan. Add leek, celery, carrots and garlic and sauté for 3-4 minutes. Add dal, kombu stock and water and bring to a boil. Reduce heat and simmer for 30 minutes or until dal is tender.

Reserve ¼ cup of the coconut milk and put it in a small saucepan. Now add the rest of the can of coconut milk to the soup along with the lemon juice.

Heat the ¼ cup coconut milk over medium heat and add

the chili paste, whisking until paste is completely dissolved. Stir this mixture into soup pot thoroughly, heating through. Taste for spiciness and for salt and pepper. If you think it needs more spice, take out some of the hot soup liquid, put it in the small saucepan and dissolve more chili paste into it. Then add that to the pot. In other words, don't add a blop of chili paste into the soup without making sure it is dissolved first. This is not something you want to take a big bite of, for sure! And yes, I am speaking from experience!

When ready to serve, remove Kombu and serve in bowls with a ½ cup baby spinach leaves on the bottom. The hot soup will wilt the greens.

**Thai chili paste is found in the international section of the store. It is very spicy, so add a very small amount at a time until desired spiciness is reached.

Vegetarian Gumbo

Serves 4-6

Cooking 101: A roux (pronounced rue) is a mixture of oil and flour that is heated until it gets brown and nutty. It burns easily, so it requires constant attention, but the results are worth it!

To save time, start this recipe by getting the roux cooking and then cut your vegetables while it is cooking over LOW heat. Serve this delicious stew with cornbread if desired.

Nutrition All Star: Collard greens are an amazing green, full of antioxidants and minerals. They are one of my favorite user friendly greens since they are so easy to clean and cut. They are perfect in this gumbo!

¼ cup olive oil

¼ cup all purpose flour (**See below for gluten free version)

1 onion, chopped

1 red pepper, chopped

2 stalks celery, chopped

2 cloves garlic, minced

4 cups vegetable broth

1-15 oz can crushed tomatoes

2 bay leaves

1 teaspoon dried thyme

½ teaspoon black pepper

¼ teaspoon cayenne (or more or less to taste)

1 15-oz can kidney beans, drained

1 bunch collard greens (or another leafy green), cut into pieces

Sea salt to taste

Tabasco sauce to taste

Gather all ingredients. To make a roux, combine oil and flour in a heavy soup pot. Cook over low heat, stirring with wooden spoon or wire whisk, until it reaches a light brown color, about 15 minutes, being very careful not to burn. Meanwhile, chop onion, pepper, celery and garlic, but remember to stir the roux as well!

Slice the leafy greens. When roux is done, add chopped onion, bell pepper, celery, and garlic, and continue stirring about 2 minutes until vegetables have been coated with the roux and are beginning to soften. Add vegetable broth and whisk until roux is dissolved. Add crushed tomatoes, dried spices, kidney beans and collard greens. Simmer for 20 minutes, or until greens are wilted.

Before serving, remove bay leaf, season to taste with salt and pepper and Tabasco if desired.

**Gluten Free? No Worries! Instead of all-purpose flour, use an all-purpose gluten free mix (I like Bob's Red Mill) in the same amount. Follow directions for the roux as written. Reduce the amount of vegetable broth to 3 cups. Enjoy!

Chickpea and Sweet Potato Curry

Serves 4-6

Coconut milk really gives me a yummy feeling plus I love the sweetness of sweet potatoes, which are loaded with vitamins in this dish. The chickpeas provide great texture and great fiber!

2 Tablespoons unrefined coconut oil

1 medium onion, chopped

1 red pepper, chopped

1 (1–inch) piece fresh ginger, minced

2 cloves garlic, minced

1 large sweet potato, peeled and cut into small chunks

¼ teaspoon red chili flakes

1 cup vegetable stock

1 15–oz can coconut milk

1 teaspoon tamari

1 15–oz can chickpeas, drained

½ cup chopped fresh basil

juice from half a lime

In a large saucepan over medium-high heat, warm the oil. Add the onion, pepper, ginger, garlic and saute stirring occasionally, until the onion and pepper soften, about 5 minutes.

Add the sweet potato chunks, red pepper flakes and stir and sauté for about 1 minute. Add vegetable stock, coconut milk and chickpeas and bring to a boil, then reduce heat and simmer until sweet potatoes are tender (depending on the size of your chunks (10-20 mins). Add tamari, basil and lime juice, simmer for 5 minutes and serve.

Main Dishes/Entrees
Gingery Brown Rice Bowls

Serves 4

This recipe was inspired by the frozen rice bowls you can buy at the store. These are cheaper and taste better (in my humble opinion)!

2 cups cooked brown rice

1 Tablespoon unrefined coconut oil

2 cloves garlic, minced

1 Tablespoon minced fresh ginger (like a 2 inch slice)

2 carrots, grated or finely chopped (grate in your food processor if you have one)

2 heads bok choy, washed and sliced

1 15 oz can Westbrae Soybeans, drained

1½ Tablespoons tamari

1½ Tablespoons mirin

Sesame seeds for garnish

Melt oil in a skillet over medium heat and add garlic, ginger and carrots, and sauté for 5-7 minutes or until carrots are tender (this is one of my favorite ways to eat carrots and beets, grated and sautéed in coconut oil... take a taste of these carrots- they kind of melt in your mouth–YUM!)

Sorry, I digress–now add bok choy, soy beans, tamari and mirin. Saute for 5 more minutes or until bok choy has wilted. Serve over brown rice in bowls and sprinkle with sesame seeds, if desired.

Kale and Cashew Curry over Millet

Serves 6

This recipe is really soothing. Millet is an alkaline forming grain that is easy to digest and coconut milk is creamy and comforting. Plus, you can have it on the table in 20 minutes, start to finish.

- 1 Tablespoon unrefined coconut oil

- 1 red onion, thinly sliced

- 2 portabello mushroom caps, thinly sliced

- 1 head red kale, thinly sliced

- 1 15-oz can organic coconut milk

- ½ teaspoon thai red chili paste**

- 1 teaspoon tamari

- 1 cup raw cashews

- 1 Tablespoon fresh lime juice and lime wedges for garnish

Melt coconut oil in a large soup pan over medium heat. Add onion and mushrooms and sauté until onion is clear, about 3 minutes. Add kale and cook, stirring occasionally until kale is wilting, about 5 minutes. Add coconut milk and stir to combine. Now, push the veggies to the side and add the curry paste to the pot, stirring really well to make sure it is dissolved. Stir in tamari, cashews and lime juice. Simmer for 5 minutes more and serve with lime wedges over millet.

**Chili paste is really spicy, start with a small amount and taste for spiciness. You can always add more but can't take it out once it is there, so go easy!

Millet

1 cup millet

2 cups water

1 pinch of salt

Stir millet and water together, and bring to a boil. Reduce to a simmer, cover, and cook 15-20 minutes, or until millet is cooked through (no longer though). Or, prepare using a rice cooker.

Tofu and Mushroom Masala

Serves 4-6

2 Tablespoons coconut oil

1 small yellow onion, chopped

2 cloves garlic, minced

2 fresh Anaheim chilies, seeded and chopped (these are the long, thin green ones)

16 oz extra firm tofu, cut into chunks

1 Tablespoon tamari

½ lb white button mushrooms, cut in half

2 teaspoons ground cumin

2 teaspoons chili powder

1 teaspoon paprika

1 teaspoon turmeric

3 small tomatoes, finely chopped

salt and pepper to taste

½ cup fresh cilantro, chopped

In a large skillet with a lid, melt the coconut oil over medium heat. Add the onions, garlic and chilies and cook for 3-5 minutes or until onion is clear. Add the tofu chunks and tamari and stir to coat. Cook for a few minutes more.

Add the mushrooms and the spices, stirring so spices are incorporated. Cover and cook for 3-5 minutes. Meanwhile, chop tomatoes and add them and any liquid they release to the pan along with a sprinkle of salt and pepper. Again, cover, lower the heat and cook for about 10 minutes until the mixture is liquidy. Keep the mixture simmering on low until ready to serve (the longer it simmers the more flavor the tofu will have- but it is ready to eat now.)

When ready to serve, remove from the heat and stir in the fresh cilantro and enjoy with brown rice! YUM!

Lentil Goulash

Serves 6

Did anyone else eat Hamburger Helper growing up? My mom only really made it when she was going out for the evening but I really looked forward to it. Maybe it was thinking of the little white glove dancing on the counter, who knows? Here is my version made with fiber filled lentils and healthy kamut elbows.

Nutrition All Star: Kamut is an ancient relative of modern durum wheat. It is higher in protein and minerals than "regular" wheat. Try it for a change of pace and you may not go back to regular pasta!

1 Tablespoon olive oil

1 yellow onion, chopped

2 stalks celery, chopped

½ pound cremini mushrooms

½ teaspoon basil leaves

1 teaspoon Italian Seasoning

1 15-oz can lentils, drained

1 15-oz can plum tomatoes

½ cup water

1½ cups kamut elbows (or other small pasta)

salt and pepper to taste

Heat the oil over medium heat in a large saucepan. Sauté onions, celery and mushrooms until onions are clear, about 3-5 minutes. Add basil and italian seasoning and sauté 1 minute more. Stir in the lentils and tomatoes (with the liquid), breaking up the tomatoes with the back of a spoon. Now, add water and pasta and a sprinkle of salt and pepper, bring the mixture to a boil, then reduce heat and simmer, covered, stirring occasionally, until the pasta is tender, about 20 minutes. Season to taste with salt and pepper and serve.

Buttery Cabbage and White Beans over Roasted Potatoes

Serves 4-6

Start with roasted potatoes:

4 large Yukon Gold Potatoes, washed

olive oil and salt and pepper

Preheat oven to 400F. Wash potatoes and cut into wedges. Place on a baking sheet and drizzle with olive oil and sprinkle with salt and pepper. Roast in oven for 20 minutes, remove sheet and stir them around, return to oven for another 15-20 minutes or until potatoes are done.

Buttery Cabbage and White Beans

> 1 Tablespoon non-hydrogenated margarine (like Earth Balance) or olive oil
>
> 1 onion, finely chopped
>
> 2 carrots, peeled, grated
>
> 1 teaspoon caraway seed
>
> ½ small head green cabbage, about 4 cups, sliced very thinly (like you were making coleslaw)
>
> ¼ cup water
>
> 1 (15 ounce) can white beans, drained
>
> 1 Tablespoon apple cider vinegar
>
> Salt and pepper to taste

Sauté onions in mixture of oil and margarine in soup pot for 3 minutes. Add carrot and caraway seeds and cook 3 minutes more, until seeds become fragrant. Add cabbage and ¼ cup water to pot, stirring well to incorporate the mixture together and sauté for 10 minutes over medium-low heat until cabbage is cooked. Add beans and vinegar, and cook uncovered for 3-5 minutes more, or until beans are hot, season with salt and pepper and serve over roasted potato wedges.

Cooking Tip: Grated carrots are super sweet and can offset the taste of bitter when sautéed with greens and other veggies!

Roasted Cauliflower Chiocciole (Pasta)

Serves 4-6

Roasting cauliflower makes it sweet and delicious!

12 ounces rice or whole grain pasta (little shapes are best, like chiocciole), cooked according to package directions**

1 large head cauliflower, cut into small florets

Olive oil and salt and pepper

1 Tablespoon olive oil

1 medium red onion, chopped

5 garlic cloves, minced

pinch red pepper flakes

2 Tablespoons capers

1 15–oz can white beans, drained

½ cup fresh parsley, chopped

salt and pepper to taste

Preheat oven to 475 degrees. On a rimmed baking sheet, toss cauliflower with a drizzle of olive oil and sprinkle with salt and pepper. Roast on lower rack until lightly browned and tender, 20 minutes, stirring occasionally.

**Meanwhile, put pasta on to cook as directed. In a large skillet, heat oil and sauté onion, garlic, red pepper flakes, and capers for 3-5 minutes, until onion is getting clear. Add white beans and parsley and simmer on low heat.

When pasta is cooked, reserve ½ cup pasta water; drain pasta and return to pot. Add roasted cauliflower, bean/parsley mixture and ¼ cup of the reserved water and toss to combine. If desired, toss pasta with remaining cooking liquid to add more moisture. Season with salt and pepper and serve.

Green Vegetable Curry

Serves 6

1 jalapeno pepper, seeds and ribs removed, sliced

3 cloves garlic, crushed

1-inch slice fresh ginger, chopped

1 teaspoon lemon zest

1 15-oz can coconut milk

Juice from one lemon (get its zest off first)

1 bunch cilantro, chopped (chop entire bunch, stems and all!)

1 teaspoon sea salt

2 large carrots, sliced

1 sweet potato, peeled and cubed

1 head bok choy, sliced

½ pound green beans, ends trimmed, cut in 1 inch pieces

In a food processor, puree pepper, garlic, ginger, and lemon zest until chopped into fine pieces. Add coconut milk, lemon juice, and salt and blend well.

Gather vegetables and slice carrots, cube sweet potatoes. In a large skillet, combine sweet potatoes and carrots with coconut milk mixture. Bring to a boil, reduce heat to a medium, simmer and cook until potatoes are fairly softened, about 15 minutes. Add bok choy and green beans and cook 5 minutes more, or until all vegetables are tender. Serve over brown rice.

Vegetable Soba Lo Mein

Serves 4-6

This dish is SOBA good!! Soba noodles are made from buckwheat, a gluten-free grain that contains a powerful antioxidant that can help prevent cellular damage. Right on! Bring on the pasta! For the maximum benefit (and to be completely gluten free) be sure to buy 100% buckwheat soba.

8 oz soba noodles**

1 Tablespoon olive oil

1 Tablespoon ginger, minced

2 cloves garlic, minced

pinch red pepper flakes

4 scallions, sliced (reserve some of the green parts for garnish)

2 medium carrots, grated

1 red pepper, sliced

½ lb shiitake mushrooms, stems removed and caps thinly sliced

1 head napa cabbage, shredded

1 cup vegetable broth

3 Tablespoons tamari (soy sauce)

2 Tablespoons mirin (Chinese rice wine)

1 teaspoon toasted sesame oil

¼ cup sesame seeds for garnish

**Cook pasta according to package directions, and rinse with cold water to stop the cooking.

In a large skillet, heat over medium-high heat. Sauté garlic, ginger, and pepper flakes for about a minute, then add scallions, carrots, pepper, mushrooms, and cabbage. Cover and cook over medium heat, stirring occasionally for about 5-7 minutes or until vegetables are tender and cabbage is wilted.

Add the broth, tamari, mirin, sesame oil, and cooked soba noodles to the skillet. Simmer until heated through, serve garnished with sesame seeds and scallions.

Asian Green Beans and Tempeh

Serves 4

1 pound of green beans, trimmed

olive oil and salt and pepper to taste

8 oz package spicy veggie tempeh (or any variety), crumbled (easiest to do with your hands)

2 Tablespoons tamari

2 Tablespoons Chinese rice wine (mirin)

1 teaspoon agave (you could substitute honey or unrefined sugar)

¼ teaspoon paprika

dash hot pepper sauce (optional)

1 Tablespoon coconut oil

¼ cup minced shallots

1 cup vegetable broth

1 Tablespoon tamari

1 teaspoon toasted sesame oil

2 Tablespoons arrowroot

Salt and pepper to taste

Combine the grated tempeh with 2 Tbsp. tamari, mirin, agave, and paprika and let sit for 10 minutes. Preheat the broiler to high.

Toss the green beans with a few drizzles of olive oil and sprinkle with salt and pepper. Arrange the beans in one layer on a rimmed baking sheet and broil, turning occasionally, for 10 minutes to 12 minutes or until golden brown and tender.

Meanwhile, melt the coconut oil in a large skillet over medium heat and add the grated tempeh and shallots and cook for about 10 minutes, or until shallots are clear and tempeh is browned. Combine the broth, 1 Tablespoon tamari, sesame oil and arrowroot. Add to the pan and cook for 3-5 minutes or until thickened.

Add the broiled green beans and stir until they are coated with the sauce. Season to taste with salt and pepper and serve over brown rice.

Red Quinoa Pilaf with Baby Broccoli

Serves 4

Baby Broccoli is a variety of broccoli characterized by small, compact florets. It is easy to use and just requires a bit of trimming. The florets cook quickly and are really tasty!

1 Tablespoon extra virgin olive oil

1 red onion, finely diced

3 cloves garlic, minced

1 ½ cups vegetable broth

1 cup dry white wine (don't want to use alcohol? Substitute 1 cup veggie stock and add another 1 teaspoon lemon juice)

1 Tablespoon lemon juice

1 teaspoon dried tarragon

1 cup dry red quinoa

1 teaspoon sea salt, or to taste

8 oz baby broccoli, cut into florets or bite-sized pieces

1 cup tamari

roasted cashew pieces

Heat the olive oil over medium heat in a saucepan and sauté the onion and garlic for 3 minutes.

Add the vegetable broth, wine, lemon juice and tarragon and bring to a boil.

Stir in the quinoa and salt. Reduce heat and simmer covered, about 20 minutes, or most of the liquid has been absorbed.

Meanwhile, prepare the broccoli into florets or pieces, trimming away the excess.

Lay the broccoli florets overtop of the quinoa (don't mix in), cover and continue to cook (you're actually steaming the broccoli) for 5 minutes, or until the broccoli is bright green (beautiful isn't it?)

Remove pot from heat, and toss gently to combine. Season to taste with salt and pepper.

Garnish with cashews before serving.

30-Day Meal Plan

Day 1
This week's healthy fridge staple:

Prepare Black Bean Hummus

Breakfast:

Optimum Power Breakfast – 1 bowl, add soy (or rice or almond) milk

1 cup herbal tea

Mid–morning snack (10am):

1 piece of fruit, 8 oz water

¼ cup almonds

Lunch:

Black Bean Hummus, lettuce & avocado (onions, tomato and onions optional) wrap on whole grain tortilla

1 piece of fruit, 8 oz water

Afternoon Snack (3pm):

½ cup almonds, 8 oz water

Dinner:

Easy Vegetable and Cashew Stir Fry over Brown Rice

2 oz dark chocolate, 8 oz water

Plan ahead:

Pack up single servings of stir-fry and rice for tomorrow's lunch

Day 2

Breakfast:
Super Smoothie

1 cup herbal tea

Mid-morning snack (10am):
1 piece of fruit, 8 oz water

¼ cup raisins

Lunch:
Leftover Stir Fry from last night

1 piece of fruit, 8 oz water

Afternoon Snack (3pm):
½ cup raisins or dried cranberries, 8 oz water

Dinner:
Black Bean "Enchiladas": Take 4 corn tortillas and spread 1 TBSP black bean hummus inside and roll up. Cover in parchment and cook for 10 minutes, until heated through and serve with salsa and avocado slices.

2 oz dark chocolate, 8 oz water

Plan Ahead:
Freeze leftovers in single servings for lunch later this week

Day 3

Breakfast:

2 slices whole grain bread with peanut butter

1 cup herbal tea

Mid-morning snack (10am):

1 piece of fruit, 8 oz water

4 dried apricots

Lunch:

Salad:

dark leaf lettuce with walnut pieces, raisins, dried cranberries, slice apple pieces, chopped red onion (optional) and garbanzo beans

Dressing:

1 TBS olive oil

1 TBS balsamic vinegar

1 TBS Annie's Goddess Dressing

1 piece of fruit, 8 oz water

Afternoon Snack (3pm):

6-8 dried apricots, 8 oz water

Dinner:

2 slices Italian-style Tofu Pizza

2 oz dark chocolate, 8 oz water

Day 4

Breakfast:

1½ cups cooked oatmeal. Add raisins, dried dates and walnut pieces. Sweeten with honey and brown sugar or maple syrup. Use soy, almond or rice milk.

1 cup herbal tea

Mid-morning snack (10am):

1 piece of fruit, 8 oz water

¼ cup cashews

Lunch:

Leftover Pizza from last night

1 piece of fruit, 8 oz water

Afternoon Snack (3pm):

½ cup cashews, 8 oz water

Dinner:

Curried Red Lentil Soup

1 slice whole grain bread with Earth Balance Spread

2 oz dark chocolate, 8 oz water

Plan Ahead:

You will make enough for dinner tomorrow evening

Day 5

Breakfast:

Optimum Power Breakfast cereal – 1 bowl, add soy, almond, or rice milk.

1 cup herbal tea

Mid–morning snack (10am):

1 piece of fruit, 8 oz water

¼ cup dried pineapple

Lunch:

Leftover Black Bean Enchiladas (leftover from Day 2)

1 piece of fruit, 8 oz water

Afternoon Snack (3pm):

½ cup dried pineapple, 8 oz water

Dinner:

Leftover Curried Red Lentil Soup and small green salad with Tahini dressing

1 slice whole grain bread with Earth Balance Spread

2 oz dark chocolate, 8 oz water

Day 6

Breakfast:

Flax Plus Raisin Bran cereal – 1 bowl, add soy, almond or rice milk.

1 cup herbal tea

Mid-morning snack (10am):

1 piece of fruit, 8 oz water

¼ cup pistachios

Lunch:

Easy Spinach Quesadillas: Take 1 large whole grain tortilla and cut it in half.   Place 1 cup baby spinach leaves and 2 oz Follow Your Heart Cheese inside. Either microwave or heat in a skillet until cheese melts. Serve with desired salsa.

1 piece of fruit, 8 oz water

Afternoon Snack (3pm):

½ cup pistachios, 8 oz water

Dinner:

Chickpeas & Artichoke Heart Stew ** *Double this Recipe!*

1 slice whole grain bread with Earth Balance Spread

2 oz dark chocolate, 8 oz water

Plan Ahead:

Freeze stew in single serve portions for lunch later this week

Day 7

Breakfast:
2 pieces whole grain bread with peanut butter

1 cup herbal tea

Mid-morning snack (10am):
1 piece of fruit, 8 oz water

¼ cup almonds

Lunch:
Peanut Butter and Jelly on whole grain bread

1 piece of fruit, 8 oz water

Afternoon Snack (3pm):
½ cup almonds, 8 oz water

Dinner:
Split Pea Soup

1 slice whole grain bread with Earth Balance Spread

2 oz dark chocolate, 8 oz water

Plan Ahead:
You will prepare enough soup to enjoy tomorrow evening as well

Day 8

Breakfast:

1½ cups cooked oatmeal. Add raisins, dried dates and walnut pieces. Sweeten with honey and brown sugar or maple syrup. Add soy, almond or rice milk.

1 cup herbal tea

Mid-morning snack (10am):

1 piece of fruit, 8 oz water

¼ cup raisins mixed with peanuts

Lunch:

Leftover Chickpea and Artichoke Stew from Day 6 (from freezer)

1 piece of fruit, 8 oz water

Afternoon Snack (3pm):

GORP: ¼ cup raisins mixed with ¼ cup peanuts, 8 oz water

Dinner:

Leftover Split Pea Soup from last night

1 slice whole grain bread with Earth Balance Spread

2 oz dark chocolate, 8 oz water

Day 9

This Week's Healthy Fridge Staple:

Prepare Chickpea Hummus

Breakfast:

Optimum Power Breakfast cereal – 1 bowl, add soy, almond or rice milk.

1 cup herbal tea

Mid-morning snack (10am):

1 piece of fruit, 8 oz water

4 dried apricots

Lunch:

Hummus, cucumber, avocado, & Vegenaise (brand) sandwich (onion, tomato and mustard optional) on whole grain bread

1 piece of fruit, 8 oz water

Afternoon Snack (3pm):

6-8 dried apricots, 8 oz water

Dinner:

Nachos (corn tortilla chips) topped with pinto beans, guacamole, salsa, Vegan Gourmet or other soy cheese

2 oz dark chocolate, 8 oz water

Day 10

Breakfast:

Flax Plus Raisin Bran cereal – 1 bowl, add soy, almond or rice milk

1 cup herbal tea

Mid-morning snack (10am):

1 piece of fruit, 8 oz water

¼ cup cashews

Lunch:

Leftover nachos from last night

1 piece of fruit, 8 oz water

Afternoon Snack (3pm):

½ cup cashews, 8 oz water

Dinner:

Easy White Bean and Spinach Pasta

1 small green salad with Tahini dressing

2 oz dark chocolate, 8 oz water

Plan Ahead:

Pack up single serve portions of leftovers for tomorrow's lunch

Day 11

Breakfast:
2 slices whole grain bread with peanut butter

1 cup herbal tea

Mid-morning snack (10am):
1 piece of fruit, 8 oz water

¼ cup dried pineapple

Lunch:
Leftover White Bean and Spinach Pasta from last night

1 piece of fruit, 8 oz water

Afternoon Snack (3pm):
½ cup dried pineapple, 8 oz water

Dinner:
Thirty Minute Minestrone Soup

1 slice whole grain bread with Earth Balance Spread

2 oz dark chocolate, 8 oz water

Plan Ahead:
Pack single servings of this soup for lunch tomorrow

Day 12

Breakfast:

1 ½ cups cooked oatmeal. Add raisins, dried dates and walnut pieces. Sweeten with honey and brown sugar or maple syrup. Use soy, almond or rice milk.

1 cup herbal tea

Mid-morning snack (10am):

1 piece of fruit, 8 oz water

¼ cup pistachios

Lunch:

Leftover Minestrone soup and a green salad

1 piece of fruit, 8 oz water

Afternoon Snack (3pm):

½ cup pistachios, 8 oz water

Dinner:

Fragrant Rice Noodles ** *Double this Recipe!*

2 oz dark chocolate, 8 oz water

Day 13

Breakfast:

Optimum Power Breakfast – 1 bowl, add soy, almond or rice milk

1 cup herbal tea

Mid–morning snack (10am):

1 piece of fruit, 8 oz water

¼ cup almonds

Lunch:

Peanut Butter and Jelly on whole grain bread

1 piece of fruit, 8 oz water

Afternoon Snack (3pm):

½ cup almonds, 8 oz water

Dinner:

Leftover Fragrant Rice Noodles

2 oz dark chocolate, 8 oz water

Day 14

Breakfast:

Flax Plus Power Breakfast – 1 bowl, add soy, almond or rice milk

1 cup herbal tea

Mid-morning snack (10am):

1 piece of fruit, 8 oz water

¼ cup dried cranberries

Lunch:

Green Salad with 2 oz baked tofu and Tahini dressing

1 piece of fruit, 8 oz water

Afternoon Snack (3pm):

½ cup dried cranberries, 8 oz water

Dinner:

Spanish Potato Onion Soup ** *Double this Recipe*

2 slices whole grain bread with Earth Balance Spread

2 oz dark chocolate, 8 oz water

Day 15

This week's healthy fridge staple:

Prepare Sunflower Seed Pate

Breakfast:

1½ cups cooked oatmeal. Add raisins, dried dates and walnut pieces. Sweeten with honey and brown sugar or maple syrup. Add soy, almond or rice milk.

1 cup herbal tea

Mid-morning snack (10am):

1 piece of fruit, 8 oz water

4 dried apricots

Lunch:

Sunflower Seed Pate Wraps with Avocado, Tomatoes Red Onions:
2 Sprouted Whole Grain Tortillas
4 Tablespoons Sunflower Seed Pate
¼ cup thinly sliced red onion
1 Plum Tomato, sliced
½ avocado, sliced
1 handful baby greens

1 piece of fruit, 8 oz water

Afternoon Snack (3pm):

6-8 dried apricots, 8 oz water

Dinner:

Leftover Spanish Potato Onion Soup with a green salad and tahini dressing

2 oz dark chocolate, 8 oz water

Day 16

Breakfast:

Two slices whole grain bread with 2 TBSP almond butter

1 cup herbal tea

Mid-morning snack (10am):

1 piece of fruit, 8 oz water

¼ cup nuts, dried fruit or combo

Lunch:

*Sunflower Seed Pate Wraps with Avocado, Tomatoes
Red Onions:*
2 Sprouted Whole Grain Tortillas
4 Tablespoons Sunflower Seed Pate
1/4 cup thinly sliced red onion
1 Plum Tomato, sliced
½ avocado, sliced
1 handful baby greens

1 piece of fruit, 8 oz water

Afternoon Snack (3pm):

½ cup nuts, dried fruit or combo, 8 oz water

Dinner:

Smoky Black Eyed Peas and Collards

2 oz dark chocolate, 8 oz water

Plan Ahead:

Freeze leftover Smoky Black Eyed Peas in single serve portions
for lunch later this week

Day 17

Breakfast:
Super Smoothie

1 cup herbal tea

Mid–morning snack (10am):
1 piece of fruit, 8 oz water

¼ cup nuts, dried fruit or combo

Lunch:
Sunflower Seed Pate Wraps (like above if you have pate left) if not, almond butter and jelly sandwich

1 piece of fruit, 8 oz water

Afternoon Snack (3pm):
½ cup nuts, dried fruit or combo, 8 oz water

Dinner:
Coconut Vegetable Curry over Cilantro Quinoa

2 oz dark chocolate, 8 oz water

Plan Ahead:
Prepare enough to have for dinner tomorrow

Day 18

Breakfast:
Breakfast Parfait with Flaxseed Crunch

1 cup herbal tea

Mid-morning snack (10am):
1 piece of fruit, 8 oz water

1 rice cake with 1 TBSP peanut or almond butter

Lunch:
Green Salad with 2 oz baked tofu and Tahini dressing

1 piece fruit, 8 oz water

Afternoon Snack (3pm):
2 rice cakes with 1 TBSP peanut or almond butter, 8 oz water

Dinner:
Leftover Curry and Quinoa

2 oz dark chocolate, 8 oz water

Day 19

Breakfast:

1½ cups cooked oatmeal. Add raisins, dried dates and walnut pieces. Sweeten with honey and brown sugar or maple syrup. Use soy, almond or rice milk.

1 cup herbal tea

Mid-morning snack (10am):

1 piece of fruit, 8 oz water

¼ cup nuts, dried fruit or combo

Lunch:

Leftover Smoky Black Eyed Peas and Collards (from freezer)

1 piece fruit, 8 oz water

Afternoon Snack (3pm):

½ cup nuts, dried fruit or combo, 8 oz water

Dinner:

Tempeh Chili and Corn Chips

2 oz dark chocolate, 8 oz water

Plan Ahead:

Prepare enough chili to have for lunch tomorrow

Day 20

Breakfast:

Breakfast Parfait with Flaxseed Crunch

1 cup herbal tea

Mid-morning snack (10am):

1 piece of fruit, 8 oz water

1 rice cake with 1 TBSP peanut or almond butter

Lunch:

Taco salad: 1 cup leftover Tempeh Chili over 2 cups baby greens with ½ cup salsa and ½ avocado, sliced.

1 piece fruit, 8 oz water

Afternoon Snack (3pm):

2 rice cakes with 1 TBSP peanut or almond butter, 8 oz water

Dinner:

Farmstand Ratatouille with White Beans over Brown Rice

2 oz dark chocolate, 8 oz water

Plan Ahead:

Prepare 2 cups of extra rice for tomorrow night's dinner. Pack up servings of Ratatouille for tomorrow's lunch

Day 21

Breakfast:
Two slices whole grain bread with 2 TBSP almond butter

1 cup herbal tea

Mid-morning snack (10am):
1 piece of fruit, 8 oz water

¼ cup nuts, dried fruit or combo

Lunch:
Leftover Ratatouille (eat as soup) with a small green salad

1 piece fruit, 8 oz water

Afternoon Snack (3pm):
½ cup nuts, dried fruit or combo, 8 oz water

Dinner:
Rainbow Brown Rice with Almonds

2 oz dark chocolate, 8 oz water

Plan Ahead:
Prepare enough Rainbow Rice to enjoy for tomorrow evenings dinner.

Day 22

This week's healthy fridge staple:

Prepare Lentil Pate

Breakfast:

Super Smoothie

1 cup herbal tea

Mid-morning snack (10am):

1 piece of fruit, 8 oz water

¼ cup nuts, dried fruit or combo

Lunch:

Lentil Pate Sandwiches: Spread pate on 2 pieces of whole grain bread with arugula and tomatoes

1 piece fruit, 8 oz water

Afternoon Snack (3pm):

½ cup nuts, dried fruit or combo, 8 oz water

Dinner:

Leftover Rainbow Brown Rice with Almonds

2 oz dark chocolate, 8 oz water

Day 23

Breakfast:

Optimum Power Breakfast – 1 bowl, add soy (or rice or almond) milk

1 cup herbal tea

Mid-morning snack (10am):

1 piece of fruit, 8 oz water

¼ cup nuts, dried fruit or combo

Lunch:

Peanut Butter and Jelly on whole grain bread

1 piece fruit, 8 oz water

Afternoon Snack (3pm):

½ cup nuts, dried fruit or combo, 8 oz water

Dinner:

Baked potatoes with chives and 1 TBSP Earth Balance and a green salad with Tahini dressing

2 oz dark chocolate, 8 oz water

Day 24

Breakfast:
Super Smoothie

1 cup herbal tea

Mid-morning snack (10am):
1 piece of fruit, 8 oz water

1 rice cake with 1 TBSP peanut or almond butter

Lunch:
Lentil Pate Sandwiches: Spread pate on 2 pieces of whole grain bread with arugula and tomatoes

1 piece of fruit, 8 oz water

Afternoon Snack (3pm):
2 rice cakes with 1 TBSP peanut or almond butter, 8 oz water

Dinner:
Moroccan Chickpea Stew over Brown Rice

2 oz dark chocolate, 8 oz water

Plan Ahead:

Prepare enough for lunch tomorrow. Also, prepare 2 cups of extra brown rice for dinner in 2 days.

Day 25

Breakfast:

1 ½ cups cooked oatmeal. Add raisins, dried dates and walnut pieces. Sweeten with honey and brown sugar or maple syrup. Use soy, almond or rice milk.

1 cup herbal tea

Mid-morning snack (10am):

1 piece of fruit, 8 oz water

¼ cup sunflower or pumpkin seeds

Lunch:

Moroccan Chickpea Stew over Brown Rice

1 piece fruit, 8 oz water

Afternoon Snack (3pm):

½ cup sunflower or pumpkin seeds, 8 oz water

Dinner:

Easy Potato and Kale Soup

2 slices whole grain bread with Earth Balance Spread

2 oz dark chocolate, 8 oz water

Plan Ahead:

Prepare enough soup to enjoy for tomorrow evening's meal

Day 26

Breakfast:

Two slices whole grain bread with 2 TBSP almond butter

1 cup herbal tea

Mid-morning snack (10am):

1 piece of fruit, 8 oz water

¼ cup sunflower or pumpkin seeds

Lunch:

Dark leaf lettuce with walnut pieces, raisins, dried cranberries, slice apple pieces, chopped red onion (optional) and garbanzo beans

Dressing:

1 TBS olive oil

1 TBS balsamic vinegar

1 TBS Annie's Goddess Dressing

1 piece fruit, 8 oz water

Afternoon Snack (3pm):

½ cup sunflower or pumpkin seeds, 8 oz water

Dinner:

Leftover Potato and Kale Soup and a green salad

1 slice whole grain bread with Earth Balance Spread

2 oz dark chocolate, 8 oz water

Day 27

Breakfast:
Breakfast Parfaits with Flaxseed Crunch

1 cup herbal tea

Mid–morning snack (10am):
1 piece of fruit, 8 oz water

¼ cup nuts, seeds, dried fruit or combo

Lunch:
Easy Spinach Quesadillas: Take 1 large whole grain tortilla and cut it in half.   Place 1 cup baby spinach leaves and 2 oz Follow Your Heart Cheese inside. Either microwave or heat in a skillet until cheese melts. Serve with desired salsa.

1 piece fruit, 8 oz water

Afternoon Snack (3pm):
½ cup nuts, seeds, dried fruit or combo, 8 oz water

Dinner:
Rice and Lentil Burgers (use leftover rice from day 24) with Wilted Greens

2 oz dark chocolate, 8 oz water

Plan Ahead:
Freeze leftover burgers for lunch the next two days

Day 28

Breakfast:

Optimum Power Breakfast – 1 bowl, with soy (or rice or almond) milk

1 cup herbal tea

Mid-morning snack (10am):

1 piece of fruit, 8 oz water

¼ cup nuts, seeds, dried fruit or combo

Lunch:

Leftover Lentil Burgers wrapped in a whole grain tortilla with lettuce, tomato and avocados

1 piece fruit, 8 oz water

Afternoon Snack (3pm):

½ cup nuts, seeds, dried fruit or combo, 8 oz water

Dinner:

Mexican Corn Stew and a green salad

2 oz dark chocolate, 8 oz water

Plan Ahead:

Prepare enough stew to enjoy for tomorrow evening's meal.

Day 29

Breakfast:

1 ½ cups cooked oatmeal. Add raisins, dried dates and walnut pieces. Sweeten with honey and brown sugar or maple syrup. Use soy, almond or rice milk.

1 cup herbal tea

Mid–morning snack (10am):

1 piece of fruit, 8 oz water

¼ cup nuts, seeds, dried fruit or combo

Lunch:

Leftover Lentil Burgers over a green salad with Tahini dressing

1 piece fruit, 8 oz water

Afternoon Snack (3pm):

½ cup nuts, seeds, dried fruit or combo, 8 oz water

Dinner:

Leftover Mexican Corn Stew and a green salad

2 oz dark chocolate, 8 oz water

Plan Ahead:

Pack single-serve containers of soup for tomorrow's lunch

Day 30

Breakfast:
Breakfast Parfaits with Flaxseed Crunch

1 cup herbal tea

Mid-morning snack (10am):
1 piece of fruit, 8 oz water

¼ cup nuts, seeds, dried fruit or combo

Lunch:
1 whole wheat tortilla filled with hummus and avocado slices

1 piece fruit, 8 oz water

Afternoon Snack (3pm):
½ cup nuts, dried fruit or combo, 8 oz water

Dinner:
Tempeh Bolognese over Zucchini Pasta

2 oz dark chocolate, 8 oz water

Recipes for 30-Day Meal Plan

Breakfast:
Yogurt Parfaits with Flaxseed Crunch

Makes 4 parfaits

Soy yogurt is loaded with beneficial bacteria and the fruit adds sweetness and fiber. Just be sure to buy unsweetened—even if you sweeten it yourself you will generally add much less than the food companies.

2 cups unsweetened soy or rice yogurt

1 drop of stevia or agave nectar to taste

1 cup assorted berries

Mix yogurt with sweetener. In a parfait glass, layer yogurt, berries and flaxseed crunch and serve.

Flaxseed Crunch

This crunchy topping is a great source of Omega 3 fatty acids!

½ cup flaxseed, ground in a coffee grinder

½ cup walnuts, toasted and chopped

1 teaspoon cinnamon

Mix all ingredients together and store in an airtight container in the refrigerator.

Super Smoothie

> 2 Tablespoons Hemp Protein (or plant-based protein of choice)
>
> 1 teaspoon Spirulina or 1 cup fresh greens such as spinach, chard, romaine lettuce or kale
>
> ½ cup of frozen berries
>
> 1 cups unsweetened almond milk
>
> 1 banana

Blend all ingredients together in a blender until creamy and enjoy!

Days 1-7

Healthy Fridge Staple:
Black Bean Hummus

This high protein spread is delish and super easy to make. Enjoy it with vegetables for a healthy snack or wrapped in tortillas for lunch.

Note: To save money, cook your own beans with a pressure cooker. New pressure cookers have safety devices, and are very economical. Soak beans overnight to remove gas. Pour out old water and replace with fresh before cooking. Most beans cook in under 20 minutes. Pressure cookers also cook potatoes and other long-cooking vegetables in a very short time. I couldn't live without mine!

1 clove garlic, minced

1 15-oz can, or 2 cups black beans, drained, liquid reserved

1 Tablespoon tahini

¼ cup lemon juice

1 Tablespoon olive oil

½ teaspoon cumin, ground

½ teaspoon salt

¼ teaspoon cayenne pepper (or to taste)

½ teaspoon paprika

½ cup fresh cilantro

Process all ingredients in a food processor until smooth, using reserved bean liquid to thin.

Easy Vegetable Cashew Stir-Fry over Brown Rice

Serves 4

Stir-fries are a great way to eat more vegetables! You can use whatever you have on hand (read: clean out that produce drawer!).

Cook's Tip: When making a stir-fry, try to cut all of your vegetables about the same size so they cook evenly. The thickening agent in this recipe is arrowroot, a gluten-free ingredient often sold with the spices.

> 1 Tablespoon coconut oil (could use olive, just don't heat it too high)
>
> 1 onion, sliced
>
> 1 red bell pepper, sliced
>
> ½ pound broccoli florets
>
> ½ pound Crimini mushrooms, sliced
>
> 1 small head Napa cabbage, thinly sliced

SAUCE:

> 1 Tablespoon arrowroot
>
> 1/3 cup tamari or soy sauce
>
> 2/3 cup vegetable broth
>
> 2 cloves garlic, minced
>
> 1 2-inch piece of fresh ginger, minced
>
> ½ cup raw cashews

Gather ingredients. Slice onion and pepper. Also, prepare broccoli into florets, slice mushrooms and Napa cabbage.

When vegetables are ready, heat oil in heavy skillet or wok. Add onion and pepper and cook for 3 minutes. Add broccoli and mushrooms and cook for 5 minutes more. Add cabbage and cook, stirring for 2 minutes.

Meanwhile, mince garlic and ginger. In a small bowl, mix together the arrowroot, tamari, vegetable broth, ginger, and garlic. Whisk until smooth. Pour sauce over vegetable mixture, stirring constantly.

When sauce has thickened (about 2 minutes), stir in cashews and serve immediately.

Brown Rice:

>1 cup short grain brown rice
>
>2 cups water
>
>1 pinch of salt

Stir rice and water together, and bring to a boil. Reduce to a simmer, cover, and cook 40-50 minutes, or until rice is cooked through (no longer tough). Or, prepare using a rice cooker.

Curried Red Lentil Soup

Serves 6

This soup is the ultimate in comfort food! The coconut milk is creamy and the spices are satisfying! Oh, and it is good for you (of course!) — the lentils are high in fiber and protein. Serve this with a green salad and a flatbread or pitas.

Note: Soak lentils in water overnight (or at least 3 hours) & drain to remove gas.

2 Tablespoons unrefined coconut oil

1 medium onion, chopped

3 cloves garlic, minced

1 teaspoon garam masala

½ teaspoon chili powder

1 teaspoon cumin

1 28 oz can diced tomatoes

1 cup red lentils

2 cups vegetable broth

1 ½ cups coconut milk

2 teaspoons lemon juice

3 cups baby spinach

salt and pepper to taste

Gather all ingredients. Chop onion and mince garlic.

Heat oil in a large saucepan. Add onion and garlic and sauté for 3-4 minutes. Add spices and cook for one minute. Add tomatoes, lentils, broth or water and bring to a boil. Reduce heat and simmer for 30 minutes or until lentils are tender.

Before serving, stir in coconut milk, lemon juice and baby spinach just until it wilts and add salt and pepper to taste.

Creamy Split Pea Soup

Serves 4-6

Yum! This creamy soup is really satisfying, loaded in fiber and protein. Don't leave out the parsnip—it adds great sweetness to balance the split peas. Also, fresh thyme really makes a difference in this recipe.

Note: Soak peas overnight & drain to remove gas.

1 Tablespoon olive oil

2 medium carrots, finely chopped

2 stalks celery, finely chopped

1 parsnip, finely chopped

1 onion, finely chopped

2 cups green split peas, rinsed and picked over

4 cups vegetable stock

4 cups water

1 Tablespoon fresh thyme, minced

1 bay leaf

salt and black pepper to taste

Heat oil in a large saucepan over medium heat. Stir in carrot, celery, parsnip, and onion, and sauté until softened (8-10 minutes), stirring occasionally. Add split peas, stock, water, thyme, and bay leaf. Bring mixture to a boil, cover, and reduce heat to simmer. Cook until split peas are very tender, about 50 minutes to an hour (less time if soaked).

Remove bay leaf. Transfer mixture to a food processor, or blender, and pulse until almost smooth.

Return to pot and heat until hot, season with salt and pepper and serve. This soup is thick and creamy, but feel free to add more water if you would like it to be thinner. You may need to adjust the seasonings.

Days 8-15

Healthy Fridge Staple:

Chickpea Hummus

This high protein spread is simple to make and great to have on hand to keep you full.

1 15-oz. can or 2 cups chickpeas, drained

2 crushed garlic cloves

½ teaspoon salt

¼ cup lemon juice

2 Tablespoons olive oil

2 Tablespoons tahini

1 teaspoon dried dill

Puree all the ingredients in a food processor or blender until creamy. Add additional oil, if necessary for desired consistency.

White Bean and Garlic Sauce Over Brown Rice Pasta

Serves 4

White beans provide the base for a creamy, garlicky white sauce, adding protein and fiber to this dish. Serve this over brown rice pasta for a nice change from wheat pastas.

For a complete meal--Serve with a green salad.

Cook's Tip: When a recipe calls for fresh parsley, dried really won't cut it. Also, my favorite way to cut most fresh herbs is a good pair of kitchen scissors. They are a great addition to your kitchen — you can snip the oregano right into the pot!

12 oz whole grain or rice pasta spirals**

2 Tablespoons grapeseed or olive oil

1 large yellow onion, finely chopped

5 garlic cloves, thinly sliced

2-15 ounce cans, or 4 cups cannelini (white kidney) beans, drained and rinsed

2 cups vegetable broth

1 Tablespoon fresh oregano (or 2 teaspoons dried)

¼ cup fresh parsley

1 Tablespoon lemon juice

Sea salt and black pepper to taste

**Cook pasta first according to package directions. Do not overcook it since you will be heating up again with the sauce. Rinse it under cold water when it is done to stop the cooking.

Gather all ingredients. Chop onions and slice garlic.

Heat the oil in a medium saucepan. Add the onions and cook over medium-low heat for about 7 minutes, or until the onions are softened and starting to brown. Add the garlic, beans, broth, and oregano and cook for a few more minutes, until fragrant.

Add the parsley, lemon juice, salt, and pepper to taste. To make the sauce "creamy" mash down about half of the beans using a potato masher or an immersion blender. Toss with cooked pasta spirals and serve. Or, you can enjoy it as-is.

Thirty-Minute Minestrone Soup

Serves 6

This tomato-based soup is easy to make and freezes well. The white beans provide fiber and protein to fill you up. This soup is great as the seasons change. It is light so you can enjoy it on a warmer day with a green salad. But, it is also hearty enough to take a chill off of a cold night, especially if served with a hearty, sprouted grain bread.

Time Saver: Since this soup freezes well, why not make a double batch and freeze individual containers to take for lunch?

1 Tablespoon grapeseed or olive oil

1 leek, washed and sliced**

3 stalks celery, sliced

1 garlic clove, minced

2 medium zucchini, sliced

1 quart water or vegetable broth

1 bay leaf

1 teaspoon Italian seasoning

1 28-ounce can diced tomatoes

1 15-ounce can white beans

Salt and freshly ground black pepper

Gather all ingredients. Wash and slice the leek. Mince garlic, slice celery, and zucchini. Heat the oil in a soup pot, and add the leek, celery, garlic, and zucchini and sauté for 3-5 minutes. Add water or vegetable broth, add bay leaf and Italian seasoning.

Add canned tomatoes and beans with their liquid to soup pot. Cover, bring to a boil, reduce heat and simmer for 10-15 minutes, or until vegetables are tender (time depends on the size of your vegetable pieces).

Discard bay leaf, add salt and pepper to taste, and spoon into bowls to serve.

**Never used a leek? It looks like a huge green onion. To clean and cut it--cut it off at about half way where the green stalks are getting tough. Now, cut the leek in quarters while keeping the root intact. Slice thinly and place in a colander to clean the pieces thoroughly to remove sand and grit found inside the leek.

Days 16-22

Healthy Fridge Staple:

Sunflower Seed Pate

This raw spread is so delicious! Sunflower seeds are a great source of protein and are loaded with B vitamins and minerals. This is a great spread to enjoy with vegetables, or a filling for sandwiches.

1½ cups raw sunflower seeds, soaked overnight*

½ cup lemon juice

4 scallions, chopped

¼ cup tahini

¼ cup tamari (soy sauce)

½ cup fresh parsley, chopped

2 cloves garlic, minced

½ teaspoon cayenne pepper (or more to taste)

In a food processor, process the soaked sunflower seeds, lemon juice, scallions, tahini, tamari, parsley, garlic, and cayenne until the mixture is a smooth paste. Season to taste, adding more tamari or cayenne as needed.

*Soaking the seeds overnight makes them more digestible and easier to blend into a creamy paste. Discard soaking water and rinse seeds, removing hulls that have come off. If you don't have time, you can soak for an hour instead.

Tempeh Chili

Serves 4-6

This recipe uses grated tempeh to replace ground meat. Tempeh is a cultured food made from soybeans. Using canned beans makes this a quick and easy recipe. Serve as is or prepare it on top of a salad for a healthy version of a taco salad.

8 ounces tempeh, any variety

1 Tablespoon olive oil

1 onion, chopped

1 red pepper, chopped

1 jalapeño pepper, seeded and diced

3 cloves garlic, minced

1 28-ounce can whole plum tomatoes

1 15-ounce can black beans, drained and rinsed

2 15-ounce cans kidney beans, drained and rinsed

1 teaspoon cumin

1 Tablespoon chili powder

dash cayenne pepper

2 Tablespoons apple cider vinegar

Crumble or grate tempeh into small pieces using your hands or a grater. Set aside. In a large saucepan, heat the oil over medium high heat. Sauté onions and red and jalepeno peppers in oil until onions are clear. Add garlic cloves and grated tempeh and cook, stirring often, for 5 minutes until tempeh is starting to brown. Add tomatoes and break them up into the tempeh using the back of a wooden spoon. Add remaining ingredients and bring to a boil.

Reduce heat, and simmer for at least 20 minutes before serving.

Smokey Black Eyed Peas and Collards

Serves 4

Black-Eyed Peas are a fantastic source of protein and fiber and collard greens are packed with anti-oxidants and vitamins. The smokey tempeh strips give it a bacon-like flavor, but tempeh is a whole, healthy food, unlike some of the other "fake" bacons.

I like to serve this dish with brown rice, so that is what I am including here. But, it is also great with cornbread or just as it is!

1 6-oz package Lightlife Smoky Tempeh Strips, diced

2 Tablespoons olive oil

3 cloves garlic, minced

1 medium onion, sliced

1 red pepper, chopped

1 15-oz can, or 2 cups black eyed peas, drained

1 bunch collard greens, sliced into small pieces

1 pinch crushed red pepper flakes

1 teaspoon salt

½ teaspoon black pepper

1 cup vegetable broth

Gather all ingredients. Dice tempeh strips, mince the garlic, and slice the onion, red pepper and collard greens.

In a large soup pot, heat oil and cook tempeh, garlic, onions and red pepper until onions are clear and tempeh is browned. Add peas, collards, seasonings and broth and simmer until collards are tender, about 20 minutes.

Brown Rice

1 cup short grain brown rice

2 cups water

1 pinch of salt

Stir rice and water together, and bring to a boil. Reduce to a simmer, cover, and cook 40-50 minutes, or until rice is cooked through (no longer tough). Or, prepare using a rice cooker.

Easy Vegetable Coconut Curry With Cilantro Quinoa

Serves 4

1 Tablespoon olive oil

1 onion, sliced

2 cloves garlic, minced

1 14-ounce can organic coconut milk

1 Tablespoon red curry paste**

¼ cup vegetable stock

1/3 cup water

1 cup broccoli florets

2 carrots, sliced

1 cup sliced Cremini mushrooms

3 cups baby spinach

¼ cup lime juice

salt and pepper to taste

**If this is your first time using curry paste, start with a smaller amount and increase gradually to desired spice level.

In a large skillet or wok, heat oil and sauté onions and garlic until clear. Push to the sides of the pan. Spoon about 1/3 cup of the coconut milk into the skillet. Add the chili paste and cook the mixture, whisking, for 1 minute, or until chili paste is dissolved. Add the rest of the coconut milk, stock, water and all vegetables, except spinach and simmer the mixture for 5 minutes, or until vegetables are crisp-tender. Add spinach in batches, stirring until each batch is wilted. Right before serving, add lime juice and salt and pepper to taste.

Cilantro Quinoa

Serves 4

Cilantro is a cleansing herb. In fact, some studies show it can rid the body of mercury and other heavy metals. It is wonderful in this flavorful quinoa pilaf. Rinse dry quinoa before using to remove it's bitter coating.

1 cup fresh cilantro leaves, packed

2 cloves garlic, chopped

1 fresh jalapeño pepper, stemmed, and chopped

½ teaspoon ground cumin

¼ cup vegetable broth

2 teaspoons olive oil

2 cups vegetable broth or water

1 cup quinoa, rinsed

1 teaspoon sea salt

In a food processor or blender, blend cilantro, garlic, jalapeño pepper, cumin and ¼ cup broth until smooth. With motor running, gradually add olive oil until mixture is smooth and well-blended.

In a saucepan over medium heat, stir together 2 cups of stock or water, rinsed quinoa, cilantro mixture and salt. Cover, bring to a boil over high heat, then reduce heat and simmer until liquid is absorbed, about 15 minutes. Season with additional salt if needed and serve.

Rainbow Brown Rice Sauté

Serves 4

This dish is a study in color! Grating your carrots and beets allows the sweetness and color to "infuse" this dish.

Time Saver: If you have a food processor, use to grate your carrots and beets.

   1 Tablespoon unrefined coconut oil

   2 cloves garlic, minced

   1 teaspoon minced ginger

   3 green onions, sliced (use the rest of the bunch from earlier this week)

   1 yellow pepper, diced

   2 carrots, grated

   1 beet, grated

   1 Tablespoon tamari

   1 teaspoon toasted sesame oil

   1½ cups leftover short grained brown rice, cold

   ½ cup chopped cilantro

   Salt and freshly ground pepper to taste

   1 cup raw cashews, chopped

Gather all ingredients and mince garlic and ginger. Slice onion and celery. Cut pepper. Grate carrots and beets.

Heat oil in a large frying pan or wok over medium heat. Add the garlic, ginger, onions, and pepper, stirring for 2 minutes. Add the grated carrots and beets and sprinkle in tamari and sesame oil, and cook for 3-5 minutes.

Meanwhile, chop cilantro. Add the cold rice and cilantro to the skillet, using the back of a wooden spoon to break up the grains and cook until heated through, about 5 minutes. Add cashews, season with salt and pepper and serve.

Farmstand Ratatouille with White Beans

Serves 4-6

A traditional ratatouille recipe gets a protein boost from white beans.

2 Tablespoons olive oil

2 cloves garlic, minced

1 large onion, thinly sliced

1 small eggplant, cubed

1 green bell pepper, coarsely chopped

4 large tomatoes, coarsely chopped, or 2 cans (15 ounces each) diced tomatoes

3 small zucchini, cut into ¼-inch slices

1 15-oz can, or 2 cups white (like navy) beans

1 teaspoon dried leaf basil

1 teaspoon dried leaf oregano

½ teaspoon dried leaf thyme

¼ cup chopped fresh parsley

In a 4-quart Dutch oven or saucepan, heat olive oil over medium heat. Add garlic and onions and cook, stirring often, until softened, about 6 to 7 minutes. Add eggplant; stir until coated with oil. Add peppers; stir to combine. Cover and cook for 10 minutes, stirring occasionally to keep vegetables from sticking.

Add tomatoes, zucchini, beans and dried herbs; mix well. Cover and cook over low heat about 15 minutes, or until eggplant is tender. Add fresh parsley and serve.

Days 23-30

Healthy Fridge Staple:

Pumpkin Seed and Lentil Spread

Makes about 2 cups of spread

This spread is really yummy and a great source of protein. Pumpkin seeds are a good source of zinc which helps build immunity. Try this spread on a brown rice tortilla with baby spinach and tomatoes for a tasty lunch.

1 cup raw pumpkin seeds, soaked overnight*

2 cloves garlic, minced

¼ cup lemon juice

½ cup chopped scallions

¼ cup tahini

¼ cup tamari

1 15-oz can lentils, drained

½ cup fresh parsley, chopped

In a food processor, process the soaked pumpkin seeds with the garlic and lemon juice until creamy. Add scallions, tahini, tamari, lentils, and parsley until the mixture is a smooth paste.

*Soaking nuts and seeds makes them more digestible and easier to blend into a creamy spread.

Moroccan-Style Chickpea Stew Over Brown Rice

Serves 4-6

This stew is a staple in my house—quick and easy and loaded with fiber and protein. Turmeric is an anti-inflammatory spice that adds a beautiful yellow color and slightly bitter flavor.

2 Tablespoons grapeseed or olive oil

1 medium onion, chopped

3 cloves garlic, minced

1 red pepper, sliced

1 teaspoon cumin seed

½ teaspoon ground turmeric

¼ teaspoon cayenne pepper

2 15-oz cans chickpeas, drained

1 28-oz can whole plum tomatoes

¼ cup fresh lemon juice

salt and pepper to taste

Gather ingredients and put rice on to cook (see below). Chop onion and mince garlic. Slice red pepper.

Heat oil in a large saucepan. Add onion, garlic, and red pepper and sauté for 3-4 minutes. Add spices and cook for one minute. Add chickpeas and tomatoes, breaking up tomatoes with the back of a spoon and simmer on low for 10 minutes, stirring occasionally.

Before serving, add lemon juice, salt, and pepper to taste.

Brown Rice times 2

2 cups short grain brown rice

4 cups water

1 pinch of salt

Stir rice and water together, and bring to a boil. Reduce to a simmer, cover, and cook 40-50 minutes, or until rice is cooked through (no longer tough). Or, prepare using a rice cooker.

Kale and Potato Chowder

Serves 4-6

Pulsing kale in a food processor makes it very easy to disguise in soups and stews. This green flecked soup is nutrient packed and delicious. Oh, and it tastes kind of like mashed potatoes — talk about comfort food!

Time Saver! Red Potatoes are a favorite to use in most recipes since you can eat the skin. No peeling = time saved!

Nutrition All Star: White Beans are loaded with fiber and protein and help to keep you get full. In this recipe, they provide an added bonus--they are helping to make this soup creamy and rich without a lot of added fat.

1 Tablespoon grapeseed or olive oil

1 onion, diced

3 cloves garlic, minced

5 medium red potatoes, cubed, unpeeled

½ teaspoon dried rosemary

3 cups vegetable broth

2 cups water

1 15-oz can, or 2 cups, white beans, drained and rinsed

1 bunch kale, sliced very thinly (or even better, pulse it in a food processor)

Salt and pepper to taste

Gather ingredients and dice onion and mince garlic. Heat oil in a soup pot and sauté onion and garlic until tender. Meanwhile, wash and cube potatoes. Add rosemary, potatoes, broth, water, and white beans to soup pot, bring to a boil, then reduce heat to medium and cover for 20 minutes or until potatoes are tender.

Process kale through a food processor or slice thinly. Add kale to soup and cook until wilted (about 5 minutes or longer depending on size of kale pieces).

To Puree Or Not to Puree? The soup can be enjoyed as is now, filled with chunks of potatoes and beans. But, if you are in the mood for a creamy soup, that is great too! Just puree soup using an immersion blender or regular blender. Season to taste with salt and pepper and serve.

Lentil and Rice Burgers with Wilted Greens

Serves 4-6

Chef's Tip: Short-grained brown rice is the best variety to use for things that need to stick together, like burgers or croquettes. Tahini is sesame seed paste and it is what is holding these burgers together. You could substitute almond butter if you like.

Time Saver: Eden-brand canned lentils with spices added are a favorite. While dry lentils cook quickly you cannot beat these cans for a meal in minutes. Also, you should have leftover rice for this recipe, but if you don't, prepare 1 ½ cups in advance.

Lentil and Rice Burgers

Makes 6-8 burgers

1 can Eden brand lentils with onions and bay leaves, or 2 cups lentils, drained

1 cup leftover rice

2 scallions, chopped very small

1 teaspoon sea salt

½ teaspoon pepper

1 teaspoon Italian Seasoning

2 teaspoons tahini

1 teaspoon tamari (soy sauce)

½ cup rice (add at the end--needed to help it stick together)

Preheat oven to 400 F. Gather all ingredients. Using

a food processor, pulse together lentils until almost pureed. Add remaining ingredients (except last ½ cup of rice) and pulse until slightly chunky, but not pureed. Remove contents to a mixing bowl. If you don't have a food processor: In a mixing bowl, mix together lentils and 1 cup of rice. Mash together with a potato masher or a fork. The point here is to make sure the lentils are smooshy enough to hold the burgers together. When it is all mixed together, add other ingredients and mix well.

Now, add remaining ½ cup of rice to the mixture to reduce stickiness. Form mixture into patties (the mixture should be slightly sticky--make it easier to handle by lightly oiling your hands). Brush the burgers with oil (using a pastry brush). Bake on a lightly greased cookie sheet for 10 minutes, flip and bake 10 minutes more. The burgers should be holding together, but still a little soft as they will harden up after you take them out of the oven.

Wilted Greens

4 cups packed baby spinach leaves

1 Tablespoon olive or grapeseed oil

2 cloves garlic, minced

1 Tablespoon balsamic vinegar

salt and pepper to taste

Gather all ingredients. Wash spinach well and spin to dry. Place spinach leaves in a large salad bowl. In a small saucepan, heat oil and garlic. Cook on low heat for 3 to 5 minutes, until warm (you are infusing the oil with garlic, but you don't want to get it too hot). Add balsamic vinegar and whisk to blend and warm through.

Pour warm dressing over spinach and toss with tongs gently to wilt. Season with salt and pepper and serve.

Tempeh Bolognese Over Zucchini "Pasta"

Serves 4

1 large yellow onion, finely diced

1 stalk celery, finely diced

1 carrot, finely diced

4 cloves garlic, minced

1 Tablespoon olive oil

2 teaspoons dried thyme (or use 1 TBSP fresh)

1 teaspoon dried oregano

2 teaspoons dried rosemary

8 oz tempeh, crumbled

1 cup vegetable stock

1 28-ounce can Tomato Purée

3/4 cup pitted, chopped Kalamata olives

1 teaspoon salt, or to taste

1 teaspoon ground pepper

In large sauté pan or skillet, sauté onion, celery, carrot, and garlic in olive oil until onion is soft and slightly browned. Add thyme, oregano, rosemary, and crumbled tempeh, and sauté for 5 additional minutes. Add wine, tomato puree, and olives; cover and simmer sauce for 20 minutes until thickened. Add salt and pepper and serve.

Zucchini "Pasta"

Serves 4 (1 zucchini per person)

4 large zucchini

salt to taste

Bring a saucepan of salted water to a rolling boil. Slice zucchini into ribbons, using vegetable peeler or mandolin. Submerge zucchini ribbons in boiling water for 1-2 minutes, just until al-dente and drain well.

Mexican Corn Stew

Serves 6

Serve this light stew with a green salad. The fresh oregano tastes really nice in this stew but you can also use dried.

2 Tablespoons olive oil

1 red onion, sliced

1 red pepper, diced

2 cloves garlic, minced

3 cups vegetable stock

1 teaspoon cumin

1 teaspoon chili powder

1 Tablespoon fresh oregano (or 1 teaspoon dried)

¼ teaspoon cayenne pepper

½ teaspoon red pepper flakes or to taste

1 lb red potatoes, unpeeled, cut into small dice

2 cups green beans, cut in 1-inch pieces

1 28-oz can, or 3 cups, drained pinto beans

1 cup frozen corn

2 Tablespoons lime juice

½ cup cilantro, chopped

In a large saucepan, heat oil and sauté onion, red peppers, and garlic until soft, about 5 minutes. Add stock, spices, potato and green beans; cover and simmer 10 minutes.

Add the pinto beans, corn, lime juice and cilantro. Reduce heat and simmer 10 minutes, or until all the vegetables are tender.

(The following recipes are reprinted with permission from Moosewood Restaurant Cooks at Home, by The Moosewood Collective, Simon & Schuster Publishers, NY, NY, 1994.)**

Italian-Style Tofu Pizza**

Choose a Whole Wheat Pizza Crust or Dough

Topping

1½ cakes firm tofu (18 oz)

2 Tablespoons olive oil

2 teaspoons ground fennel

2 garlic cloves, minced or pressed

¼ or ½ teaspoon cayenne

1½ Tablespoon soy sauce

1 Tablespoon tomato paste

1 teaspoon dried oregano

2 cups prepared tomato sauce

salt and pepper to taste

Preheat oven according to the directions for the pizza crust or dough you are using.

Grate the tofu by hand or in a food processor, or chop it into small pea-sized pieces. Heat the oil in a large skillet and sauté the grated tofu, fennel, garlic, and cayenne for 2-3 minutes. Stir in the soy sauce, tomato paste, and oregano and continue to sauté for another minute. Add the tomato sauce, remove from the heat, and add salt and pepper to taste.

Spread the tofu topping on the pizza crust. Bake following the instructions given for the crust you are using.

Chick Pea and Artichoke Heart Stew**

    4 cups water or vegetable stock

    2 medium onions, chopped (about 1½ cups)

    2 garlic cloves, minced or pressed

    2 Tablespoons olive oil

    1 teaspoon turmeric

    1 teaspoon paprika

    4 medium red or white potatoes, cut into ½-inch cubes
        (about 4 cups)

    1 teaspoon dried rosemary

    ½ teaspoon dried sage

    1 4.5-ounce jar pureed squash baby food

    3 cups drained cooked chick peas (two 15-oz cans)

    1½ cups drained quartered artichoke hearts (14-oz
        can)

    salt and pepper to taste

In a saucepan, bring the water or vegetable stock to a
simmer. While the water heats, sauté the onions and garlic
in the oil for about 8 minutes, until soft. Stir the turmeric
and paprika into the onions and sauté for a minute. Add the
potatoes, rosemary, sage, and the simmering water or stock.
Cook for about 12 minutes, until the potatoes are tender.
Stir in the baby food squash or sweet potatoes, and add the
drained chick peas and artichoke hearts. Add salt and pepper
to taste, and return to a simmer.

Spanish Potato Onion Soup**

> 4 medium onions, halved and thinly sliced (about 4 cups)
>
> 2 Tablespoons olive oil
>
> 4 cups water
>
> 2 or 3 medium potatoes (about 4 cups sliced)
>
> 2 teaspoons paprika
>
> ½ teaspoon dried thyme
>
> 2 large bay leaves
>
> ¼ cup dry sherry
>
> 1 teaspoon salt
>
> ¼ teaspoon ground black pepper
>
> pinch of saffron

In a soup pot on medium heat, sauté the onions in the oil, stirring occasionally to prevent sticking. While they sauté, bring the water to boil in a separate pan. Cut the potatoes in half lengthwise, and then slice each half crosswise into ¼-inch-thick slices. Keeping the slices together, cut them in half lengthwise again to form wedge-shaped pieces.

When the onions are translucent, add the paprika, thyme, and bay leaves. Sauté for a minute. Pour the boiling water into the onion mixture and add the potatoes, sherry, salt and pepper. Return to a boil. Then lower the heat and simmer, covered, for about 10 minutes. Crumble in the saffron and continue to cook until the potatoes are tender. Remove the bay leaves.

Fragrant Rice Noodles with Vegetables**

   1½ quarts water
Sauce

   2 TBSP lime juice

   1 TBSP freshly grated lime peel

   ½ cup peanut butter

   2 teaspoons brown sugar

   1 cup vegetable stock

   ½ teaspoon salt

   3 garlic cloves, minced or pressed

   6 oz ¼-inch-wide rice noodles (or linguini if rice
   noodles are unavailable)

   2 leeks, well rinsed

   2 small zucchini

   2 small yellow squash

   3 TBSP vegetable oil

   ¼ cup water

In a covered pot, bring the water to a rapid boil.

Combine the sauce ingredients and mix them by hand or puree them in a blender until smooth.

When water boils, add the noodles and cook for 3-5 minutes, until just tender. Drain, rinse briefly under cool water, drain again, and set aside.

Cut the leeks, zucchini, and yellow squash into sticks 5-6 inches long and ¼ to ½ inch wide. Heat the oil in a wok or large skillet. Stir-fry the leak sticks on medium-high heat for 2 to 3 minutes. Add the zucchini and yellow squash and continue to stir-fry for about 3 to 4 minutes, until the vegetables are just tender. To prevent scorching or sticking, add about ¼ cup water while stir-frying. Add the noodles and the sauce and toss well until heated through. Serve at once.

APPENDIX

Index of High-Fiber Foods

Fruit

1 kiwi (no peel): 3 grams fiber

1 cup raw papaya: 3 grams

1 mango (no peel): 3 grams

1 cup strawberries: 3 grams

1 banana (no peel): 3 grams

1 plum with peel: 3 grams

1 nectarine with peel: 4 grams

1 cup blackberries: 8 grams

1 cup blueberries: 4 grams

1 cup cherries: 3 grams

1 peach with peel: 3 grams

1 medium apple with peel: 4 grams

1 medium orange: 4 grams

3 small apricots: 6 grams

1 pear with peel: 5 grams

1 avocado: 8 grams

1 cup dates: 13 grams

10 dried figs: 17 grams

1 cup raspberries: 8 grams

Dried Fruit

2 oz. dried apple: 4 grams

2 oz. dried apricots: 3 grams

1/4 date pieces: 3.5 grams

2 oz. dried peaches: 4 grams

2 oz. dried pineapple: 3 grams

1/2 cup dried banana slices: 4 grams

1/3 cup dried cranberries: 2 grams

1 cup sun-dried tomatoes: 7 grams

1 cup raisins: 5 grams

10 dried plums: 6 grams

10 dried peaches: 11 grams

Vegetables

1 cup cooked carrots: 5 grams

2 ears corn, cooked: 4 grams

1 large baked potato (with skin): 5 grams

1 medium sweet potato (with skin): 4–5 grams

1 cup cooked green beans: 4 grams

1 cup cooked brussels sprouts: 6.5 grams

1 artichoke: 6.5 grams

2/3 cup artichoke hearts: 6 grams

1 cup cooked broccoli: 5 grams

Beans/Lentils/Peas (cooked)

1 cup limas: 12 grams

1 cup pintos: 14 grams

1 cup garbanzos: 8 grams

1 cup kidney beans: 16 grams

1 cup black-eyed peas: 12 grams

1 cup snow peas: 4 grams

1 cup lentils: 15 grams

1 cup black beans: 15 grams

1 cup peas: 9 grams

1 cup split pea soup: 5–7 grams

Nuts/Seeds/Nut Butters

1 cup almonds: 14 grams

1 cup cashews: 4 grams

1 cup macadamia nuts: 12 grams

1 cup peanuts: 10 grams

1 cup pistachios: 14 grams

1 cup pumpkin seeds: 15 grams

1 cup sunflower seeds: 8 grams

1 cup walnuts: 6 grams

2 tablespoons natural peanut butter: 3 grams

2 tablespoons almond butter: 4 grams

1/2 cup hummus: 6 grams

Whole Grains

1 cup cooked barley: 8 grams

1 cup oatmeal: 4 grams

1 cup bulgar: 8 grams

2 buckwheat pancakes: 7 grams

1 cup brown rice: 4 grams

1 cup whole-wheat pasta noodles: 6 grams

5 cups popcorn: 6 grams

1 slice whole-grain bread: 3–5 grams

1 whole-wheat bagel: 2–3 grams

1 cup whole-grain cereal: 5–10 grams

1 oz. corn tortilla chips: 2–3 grams

1 whole-wheat tortilla: 3–5 grams

1 small corn tortilla: 2 gram

REFERENCES

Chapter 1: Happy Math

1. Burton-Freeman B, et al., "Plasma Cholecystokinin is Associated with Subjective Measures of Satiety in Women," *American Journal of Clinical Nutrition* 76 (2002) 659-67.

2. Campbell, Colin T., *The China Study* (Dallas, Texas: Benbella Books, 2004), pp.90-100.

3. Tucker LA, Thomas KS, "Increasing Total Fiber Intake Reduces Risk of Weight and Fat Gains in Women," *Journal of Nutrition* 139 (2009): 576-81.

4. Ludwig, D.S., et al., "Dietary Fiber, Weight Gain, and Cardiovascular Disease Risk Factors in Young Adults," *Journal of the American Medical Association*, 1999, 282:1539-1546.

Chapter 2: Superhero Calories

1. Kiehm T.G., et al, "Beneficial Effects of a High Carbohydrate, High Fiber Diet on Hyperglycemic Diabetic Men," *American Journal of Clinical Nutrition* 29, (1976):895-99.

2. Giacco R, et al., "Long-term Dietary Treatment with Increased Amounts of Fiber-rich Low-glycemic Index Natural Foods Improves Blood Glucose Control and Reduces the Number of Hypoglycemic Events in Type 1 Diabetic Patients," *Diabetes Care* 23 (2000):1461-66.

3. Singh, P.N., et al., "Dietary Risk Factors for Colon Cancer in a Low-Risk Population," *American Journal of Epidemiology* 148 (1998):761-74.

4. Jacobs EJ, White E., "Constipation, Laxative Use, and Colon Cancer among Middle-aged Adults," *Epidemiology* 9 (1998):385-91.

5. Lipski, Elizabeth, *Digestive Wellness* (Los Angeles: Keats Publishing, 2000), pp. 82-83.

6. Ibid.

Chapter 3: Filling Calories

1. Batterham, R., et al., "Inhibition of Food Intake in Obese Subjects by Peptide YY," *New England Journal of Medicine* 359 (2003):941-48.

2. Mattes RD, Kris-Etherton PM, Foster G, "Impact of Peanuts and Tree Nuts on Body Weight and Healthy Weight Loss in Adults," *Journal of Nutrition* 138 (2008):1741S-1745S.

3. Jenkins D et al., "Possible Benefit of Nuts in Type 2 Diabetes", *Journal of Nutrition* 138 (2008): 1752S-1756S. Penny M. Kris-Etherton PM et al., "The Role of Tree Nuts and Peanuts in the Prevention of Coronary Heart Disease: Multiple Potential Mechanisms," *Journal of Nutrition* 138 (2008): 1746S-1751S.

4. Virginia Worthington, "Nutritional Quality of Organic Versus Conventional Fruits, Vegetables, and Grains," *The Journal of Alternative and Complementary Medicine* 7 (2001):161-73.

5. Lewis V, et al., "Dietary Antioxidants and Sperm Quality in Infertile Men," *Fertility and Sterility* 86 (2006):364.

6. Chavarro, Jorge E., Willett, Walter C., Skerrett, Patrick J., *The Fertility Diet* (New York: McGraw-Hill, 2007).

Chapter 4: Nutritious Calories

1. Nielsen, FH, Milne, DB, "A Moderately High Intake Compared to a Low Intake of Zinc Depresses Magnesium Balance and Alters Indices of Bone Turnover in Postmenopausal Women," *European Journal of Clinical Nutrition* 58 (2004): 703–710. Schiller L, et al., "Effect of the Time of Administration of Calcium Acetate on Phosphorus Binding," *New England Journal of Medicine* 320 (1989):1110-13. Hallberg L, et al., "Calcium and Iron Absorption: Mechanism of Action and Nutritional Importance," *European Journal of Clinical Nutrition* 46 (1992):317-27. Clarkson E.M., et al., "The Effect of a High Intake of Calcium on Magnesium Metabolism in Normal Subjects and Patients with Chronic Renal Failure," *Clinical Science* 32 (1967):11-18.

2. British Medical Journal online publication, 15 January 2008: www.bmj.com/cgi/content/full/bmj.39440.525752.BEv1

3. Editorial, "The Antioxidant Supplement Myth," *American Journal of Clinical Nutrition* 60 (1994):157-8.

4. Marshall TG., "Vitamin D Discovery Outpaces FDA Decision Making," *Bioessays* 30 (2008):173-82.

5. Stanford Prevention Research Center, Department of Medicine Web Site (2008): www. prevention.stanford.edu

Chapter 5: The Truth about Sugar and Starch

1. McCann, Donna, et al., "Food Additives and Hyperactive Behaviour in 3-Year-Old and 8/9-Year-Old Children in the Community: a Randomised, Double-Blinded, Placebo-Controlled Trial," *The Lancet* 370 (2007):1560 – 67; see also Boris M, et al., "Foods and Additives are Common Causes of the Attention Deficit Hyperactive Disorder in Children," *Annals of Allergy* 72 (1994):462-8.

Chapter 6: Beans are the New Meat

1. Bengoa, J.M., "Recent Trends in the Public Health Aspects of Protein-Calorie Malnutrition," *World Health Organization Report, Geneva* (1970):10. No. 454, p.10.

2. Weikert C, et al., "The Relation Between Dietary Protein, Calcium and Bone Health in Women: Results from the EPIC-Potsdam Cohort," *Annals of Nutrition and Metabolism* 49 (2005):312-8; see also Sellmeyer DE, et al., "A High Ratio of Dietary Animal to Vegetable Protein Increases the Rate of Bone Loss and the Risk of Fracture in Postmenopausal Women," *American Journal of Clinical Nutrition* 73 (2001):118-22.

3. Reddy S.T., et al., "Effect of Low-Carbohydrate High-Protein Diets on Acid-Base Balance, Stone-Forming Propensity, and Calcium Metabolism," *American Journal of Kidney Diseases* 40 (2002):265-74.

4. Associated Press, "EU Scientists Confirm Health Risks of Growth Hormones in Meat," April 23, 2002.

5. Swan S.H., et al., "Semen Quality of Fertile US Males in Relation to Their Mothers' Beef Consumption During Pregnancy," Human Repro*duction*, Advanced access published on March 28, 2007.

6. National Cancer Institute Website (2008): www.cancer.gov/cancertopics/factsheet/Risk/heterocyclic-amines

7. Xu W, et al., "Nutritional Factors in Relation to Endometrial Cancer: A Report from a Population-Based Case-Control Study in Shanghai, China," *International Journal of Cancer* 120 (2007):1776-81.

8. Fontana L, et al., "Long-Term Low-Protein, Low-Calorie Diet and Endurance Exercise Modulate Metabolic Factors Associated with Cancer Risk," *American Journal of Clinical Nutrition* 84 (2006):1456-62.

9. Egeberg R, et al., "Meat Consumption, N-acetyl transferase 1 and 2 Polymorphism and Risk of Breast Cancer in Danish Postmenopausal Women," *European Journal of Cancer Prevention* 17 (2008):39-47.

10. Michaud D.S., et al., "Meat Intake and Bladder Cancer Risk in 2 Prospective Cohort Studies," *American Journal of Clinical Nutrition* 84 (2006):1177-83.

11. Campbell, *The China Study*, pp. 51-59 & pp.69-75.

Chapter 7: Whole Grains

1. Djousse L, Gaziano JM, "Egg Consumption in Relation to Cardiovascular Disease and Mortality: the Physicians' Health Study," *American Journal of Clinical Nutrition* 97(2008): 964-69.

Chapter 8: The Lowdown on Beverages

1. Bar David Y, et al., "Water Intake and Cancer Prevention" *Journal of Clinical Oncology* 22 (2004):383-85.

2. DiMeglio DP, and Mattes RD, "Liquid Versus Solid Carbohydrate: Effects on Food Intake and Body Weight," *International Journal of Obesity* 24 (2000):794–800.

3. U.S. Food and Drug Administration Website (2006): www.fda.gov/fdac/features/2006/406_sweeteners.html

4. Fincher, Cynthia E., *Healthy Living in a Toxic World* (Colorado Springs: Pinon Press, 1996), p.149.

5. Ibid. p.141.

6. Harvard Health Publications, "*Abdominal Fat and What to Do About It*," Harvard Women's Health Watch Website (2006): www.health.harvard.edu/newsweek/Abdominal-fat-and-what-to-do-about-it.htm

7. De Lange D.W., et al., "Red Wine and Red Wine Polyphenolic Compounds but Not Alcohol Inhibit ADP-Induced Platelet Aggregation," *European Journal of Internal Medicine* 14 (2003): 361-66.

Chapter 10: Why Dairy is Scary

1. Physician's Committee for Responsible Medicine Website (May 3 2007): www.pcrm.org/news/downloads/FTCTesponsetoPCRM.pdf

2. Chen H, O'Reilly E, McCullough ML, Rodriguez C, et al. "Consumption of Dairy Products and Risk of Parkinson's Disease," *American Journal of Epidemiology* 165 (2007):998-1006.

3. Stang A, Ahrens W, Baumgardt-Elms C, et al., "Adolescent Milk Fat and Galactose Consumption and Testicular Germ Cell Cancer," *Cancer Epidemiology Biomarkers and Prevention* 2006; 15 (11):2189-95.

4. Mitrou PN, Albanes D, Weinstein SJ, Pietinen P, et al., "A Prospective Study of Dietary Calcium, Dairy Products and Prostate Cancer Risk (Finland)," *International Journal of Cancer* 120 (2007):2466-73; see also Chan JM et al., "Dairy Products, Calcium, and Prostate Cancer Risk in the Physicians' Health Study," *American Journal of*

REFERENCES

Clinical Nutrition 74 (2001):549-54.

5. Fincher, *Healthy Living in a Toxic World,* p. 147.

6. Yanqiu Xia, Liji Jin, Bin Zhang, Hongyu Xue, Qiujuan Li, Yongping Xu, The Potentiation of Curcumin on "Insulin-like Growth Factor-1 in MCF-7 Human Breast Carcinoma Cells," *Life Sciences* 80 (2007):2161-69.

7. Slomiany M.G., et al., "Insulin-like Growth Factor-1 Receptor and Ligand Targeting in Head and Neck Squamous Cell Carcinoma," *Cancer Letters* 248 (2007):269-79.

8. Fürstenberger G, et al., "Serum Levels of IGF-1 and IGFBP-3 During Adjuvant Chemotherapy for Primary Breast Cancer," *The Breast* 15 (2006):64-68.

9. Figueroa J.A., et al., "Recombinant Insulin-like Growth Factor Binding Protein-1 Inhibits IGF-I, Serum, and Estrogen-dependent Growth of MCF-7 Human Breast Cancer Cells," *Journal of Cellular Physiology* 157 (1993):229-36.

10. Djavan B, Waldert M, Seitz C, Marberger M., "Insulin-like Growth Factors and Prostate Cancer," *World Journal of Urology* 19 (2001):225-33.

11. Wolk A,et al., "Insulin-like Growth Factor 1 and Prostate Cancer Risk: a Population-Based, Case-Control Study," *Journal of the National Cancer Institute* 90 (1998):911-15.

12. Aksoy Y, et al., "Serum Insulin-like Growth Factor-I and Insulin-like Growth Factor-binding Protein-3 in Localized, Metastasized Prostate Cancer and Benign Prostatic Hyperplasia," *Urologia Internationalis* 72 (2004):62-65.

13. Mawson A, et al., "Estrogen and Insulin/IGF-1 Cooperatively Stimulate Cell Cycle Progression in MCF-7 Breast Cancer Cells through Differential Regulation of c-Myc and Cyclin D1," *Molecular and Cellular Endocrinology* 229 (2005):161-73.

14. Tripkovic I, et al., "Role of Insulin-Like Growth Factor-1 in Colon Carcinogenesis: A Case-Control Study," *Archives of Medical*

Research 38 (2007):519-25

15. Ma J, Giovannucci E, Pollak M, Chan J.M., Gaziano J.M., Willett W, Stampfer M.J., "Milk Intake, Circulating Levels of Insulin-Like Growth Factor-I, and Risk of Colorectal Cancer in Men," *Journal of the National Cancer Institute* 93 (2001):1330-36.

16. Outwater J, Nicholson A, Barnard N, "Dairy Products and Breast Cancer: the IGF-I, Estrogen, and bGH Hypothesis," *Medical Hypotheses* 48 (1997):453-61.

17. Sellmeyer DE, Stone KL, Sebastian A, Cummings SR., "A High Ratio of Dietary Animal to Vegetable Protein Increases the Rate of Bone Loss and the Risk of Fracture in Postmenopausal Women," *American Journal of Clinical Nutrition* 73 (2001):118-22.

18. Weikert C, Walter D, Hoffman K, Kroke A, Bergmann MM, Boeing H, "The Relation Between Dietary Protein, Calcium and Bone Health in Women: Results from the EPIC-Potsdam Cohort," *Annals of Nutrition and Metabolism* 49 (2005):312-8.

19. Walker ARP, Walker BF, Richardson BD, "Metacarpal bone dimensions in young and aged South African Bantu consuming a diet low in calcium," *Postgraduate Medical Journal* 47 (1971):320-25. See also Campbell, *The China Study*.

20. Ibid.

21. Levy-Costa R.B., Monteiro C.A., "Cow's Milk Consumption and Childhood Anemia in the City of São Paulo, Southern Brazil," *Revista de Saúde Pública* 38 (2004): 797-803.

22. Feskanich D, Willett W C, Stampfer M J, Colditz G A, "Milk, Dietary Calcium, and Bone Fractures in Women: a 12-year Prospective Study," *American Journal of Public Health* 87 (1997):992-7.

23. Nordin BE, "Calcium and Osteoporosis," *Nutrition* 13 (1997):664-86.

24. Suzuki T, Matsuo K, Tsunoda N, et al., "Effect of Soybean on Breast Cancer According to Receptor Status: a Case-Control Study in Japan," International Journal of Cancer 123 (2008):1674-80.

25. Chang ET, Lee VS, Canchola AJ, Clarke CA, et al., "Diet and Risk of Ovarian Cancer in the California Teachers Study Cohort," *American Journal of Epidemiology* 165 (2007):802-13.

26. Kurahashi N, et al., "Soy product and Isoflavone Consumption in Relation to Prostate Cancer in Japanese Men," *Cancer Epidemiology, Biomarkers and Prevention* 16 (2007):538-45. See also Yamamoto S et al., "Soy, Isoflavones, and Breast Cancer Risk in Japan," *Journal of the National Cancer Institute* 95 (2003):1881-2. Jacobsen BK, et al., "Does High Soy Milk Intake Reduce Prostate Cancer Incidence? The Adventist Health Study (United States)," *Cancer Causes & Control* 9 (1998):553-7.

Chapter 11: Belly Fat and Blood Pressure

1. Inzitari C, et al., "Cognitive and Functional Impairment in Hypertensive Brain Microangiopathy," *Journal of the Neurological Sciences* 257 (2007):166 – 73. See also Ylikoski R, et al., "Cardiovascular Diseases, Health Status, Brain Imaging Findings and Neuropsychological Functioning in Neurologically Healthy Elderly Individuals," *Archives of Gerontology and Geriatrics* 30 (2000):115-30.

2. Kesteloot H, Joossens JV, "Relationship of Dietary Sodium, Potassium, Calcium, and Magnesium with Blood Pressure," *Hypertension* 12 (1988): 594-599. See also Houston, MC, Harper KJ, "Potassium, Magnesium, and Calcium: Their Role in Both the Cause and Treatment of Hypertension," Journal of Clinical Hypertension 10 (2008):3-11.

3. Appleby PN, Davey GK, Key TJ, "Hypertension and Blood Pressure Among Meat Eaters, Fish Eaters, Vegetarians and Vegans in EPIC-Oxford," *Public Health Nutrition* 5 (2002):645-54.

Chapter 13: Let's Get Moving

1. Esteves AM, De Mello MT, Pradella-Hallinan M, Tufik S, "Effect of Acute and Chronic Physical Exercise on Patients with Periodic Leg Movements," *Medicine & Science in Sports & Exercise* 41(2009):237-42.

2.. Passos GS, et al "Physical Exercise Can Improve Sleep Quality of Insomniac Patients?" *Associated Professional Sleep Societies Meeting* 737 (2008).

3. Bacon CG, ScD, Mittleman MA, Kawachi, I, Giovannucci E, Glasser DB, Rimm EB, "Sexual Function in Men Older Than 50 Years of Age: Results from the Health Professionals Follow-up Study," *Annals of Internal Medicine* 139 (2003):161-68.

4. Meston CM, and. Gorzalka BB, "The Effects of Immediate, Delayed, and Residual Sympathetic Activation on Sexual Arousal in Women, *Behaviour Research and Therapy* 34 (1996):143-48.

5. Dunn AL, Trivedi MH, Kampert JB, Clark CG, Chambliss HO, "Exercise Treatment for Depression: Efficacy and Dose Response," *American Journal of Preventive Medicine* 28 (2005):1-8.

6. De Moor MH, Beem AL, Stubbe JH, Boomsma DI, De Geus EJ, "Regular Exercise, Anxiety, Depression and Personality: a Population-based Study," *Preventative Medicine* 42 (2006):273-9.

7. Coulson JC, McKenna J, Field M, "Exercising at Work and Self-reported Work Performance," *International Journal of Workplace Health Management* 1 (2008):176-97.

8. University of Georgia. "Low-intensity Exercise Reduces Fatigue Symptoms By 65 Percent, Study Finds." *ScienceDaily* 2 March 2008. http://www.sciencedaily.com/releases/2008/02/080228112008.htm.

9. Steinberg H, Sykes EA, Moss T, Lowery S, LeBoutillier N, Dewey A, "Exercise Enhances Creativity Independently of Mood," *British Journal of Sports Medicine* 31 (1997):240-45.

REFERENCES

10. 55th American College of Sports Medicine Annual Meeting, Indianapolis, May 28-31, 2008. Suvi Rovio, MSc, Karolinska Institute, Stockholm, Sweden. Maria Carrillo, PhD, director of medical scientific relations, Alzheimer's Association.

11. Rutledge et al., "Social Networks and Incident Stroke Among Women With Suspected Myocardial Ischemia," *Psychosomatic Medicine* 70 (2008):282-87.

12. Glass TA, de Leon CM, Marottoli RA, Berkman LF, "Population Based Study of Social and Productive Activities as Predictors of Survival Among Elderly Americans," *British Medical Journal* 319 (1999):478-83.

13. Rose, R, "How Much Does Social Capital Add to Individual Health? A Survey Study of Russians," *Social Science & Medicine* 51 (2000):1421-35.

14. Emery CF, Hsiao ET, Hill SM, Frid DJ, "Short-term Effects of Exercise and Music on Cognitive Performance Among Participants in a Cardiac Rehabilitation Program," *Heart & Lung: The Journal of Acute and Critical Care* 32 (2003):368-73.

15. Siedliecki SL, Good M, "Effect of Music on Power, Pain, Depression and Disability," *Journal of Advanced Nursing* 54 (2006): 553-62.

16. Choi AN, Lee MS, Lim HJ, "Effects of Group Music Intervention on Depression, Anxiety and Relationships in Psychiatric Patients: A Pilot Study," *The Journal of Alternative and Complementary Medicine* 14 (2008):567-70.

17. Levitin, Daniel J, *This is Your Brain on Music* (Penguin Group, 2006).

18. Brunel University (2008, October 2). "Jog To The Beat: Music Increases Exercise Endurance By 15%," ScienceDaily.

19. Walsh JM, Rabin BS, Day R, Williams JN, Choi K, Kang JD, "The Effect of Sunlight on Postoperative Analgesic Medication Use: A Prospective Study of Patients Undergoing Spinal Surgery,"

Psychosomatic Medicine 67 (2005):156-63.

20. Ibid

21. Ulrich RS, "View Through a Window May Influence Recovery From Surgery," *Science* 224 (1984):420-21.

22. Website:
www.cchr.org/media/pdfs/Executive_Summary.pdf

23. Ibid

24. Ewing R, Schmid T, Killingsworth R, Zlot A, Raudenbush S, "Relationship Between Urban Sprawl and Physical Activity, Obesity, and Morbidity," *American Journal of Health Promotion* 18 (2003): 47-57.

25. Saelens BE, Sallis JF, Frank LD, "Environmental Correlates of Walking and Cycling: Findings from the Transportation, Urban design, and Planning Literatures, *Annals of Behavioral Medicine* 25 (2003):80-91.

26. Website:
http://archives.cnn.com/2001/CAREER/trends/08/30/ilo.study/

27. Grzywacz JG, Casey PR, Jones FA, "Workplace Flexibility and Employee Health Behaviors: A Cross-Sectional and Longitudinal Analysis," *Journal of Occupational and Environmental Medicine* 49 (2007):1302-1309.

28. Kleppa E, Sanne B, Tell GS, "Working Overtime is Associated with Anxiety and Depression: the Hordaland Health Study," *Journal of Occupational and Environmental Medicine* 50 (2008): 658-66.

29. Ko GTC, et al., "Association Between Sleeping Hours, Working Hours and Obesity in Hong Kong Chinese: the 'Better Health for Better Hong Kong' Health Promotion Campaign," *International Journal of Obesity* 31 (2007): 254-60.

Index

RECIPE LISTING

Main Dishes / Entrees

Bronwyn Schweigerdt

Bronwyn is on a mission to clear the confusion surrounding nutrition and help people live long and eat freely. When she is not flying to the rescue as Fiber-Girl, she can be found teaching seminars, researching, blogging, but mostly eating her favorite foods. She has literally helped thousands of people learn how to lose weight with her seminars and previous book: *The UnDiet: Painless Baby Steps to Permanent Weight Loss*. She has a Master's degree in nutrition from Tufts University. She lives in Sacramento, California with her chocolate eating husband and bean eating five year old daughter. People who hear her not only feel incredibly empowered and inspired, but relieved to learn how simple and fun weight loss can be!

Bronwyn also represents Compassion International as a speaker on behalf of the needy children of the world. Sponsor a child today and change their world at www.compassion.com.

For more resources from Bronwyn such as nutrition research, instructional videos, podcasts, email updates, or additional copies of this book, please visit her site at:

www.fiber-girl.com

Jennifer Brewer

Jennifer Brewer, MS, CNS is a Nutritionist and Natural Foods Chef residing in Santa Cruz, CA. She is a graduate of the Chef's Training Program at the Natural Gourmet Cookery School in New York City. Jennifer holds a Masters Degree in Nutrition and is a Certified Nutrition Specialist through the American College of Nutrition.

Jennifer is a James Beard Scholarship Recipient and has taught healthy cooking classes for a variety of organizations including the Physicians Committee for Responsible Medicine (PCRM) and the Community Alliance with Family Farmers (CAFF). Currently, Jennifer teaches a wide variety of cooking workshops and lectures, including an 8-week Natural Foods Training Course for the Home Chef, offered at New Leaf Community Markets in Santa Cruz, CA. In addition, Jennifer created a website which inspires individuals to organize their kitchen, develop time saving shopping lists and prepare delicious, unprocessed, plant based meals that everyone will enjoy.

For more of Jennifer's recipes, meal plans, email updates and blog, please visit her site at:

www.nourishingnutrition.com

A thinner, disease-free body is priceless.

Be willing to invest in your health. *You're worth it.*

Besides, sleep and water are practically free.